THE COLONIAL UNCONSCIOUS

The Colonial Unconscious

RACE AND CULTURE IN INTERWAR FRANCE

Elizabeth Ezra

CORNELL UNIVERSITY PRESS

ITHACA AND LONDON

First published 2000 by Cornell University Press
First printing, Cornell Paperbacks, 2000

Printed in the United States of America

Library of Congress Cataloging-in-Publication Data

Ezra, Elizabeth, b. 1965
    The colonial unconscious : race and culture in interwar France / Elizabeth Ezra.
        p.   cm.
    Includes bibliographical references and index.
    ISBN 0-8014-3726-1 (cloth) — ISBN 0-8014-8647-5 (paper)
        1. Indigenous peoples—France—Colonies.   2. France—Colonies—Race
    relations.   3. France—Politics and government—1914–1940.   I. Title

JV1835 .E97 2000
305.84′1′009042—dc21

                                                                                99-087707

Cornell University Press strives to use environmentally responsible suppliers and materials to the fullest extent possible in the publishing of its books. Such materials include vegetable-based, low-VOC inks, and acid-free papers that are recycled, totally chlorine-free, or partly composed of nonwood fibers. Books that bear the logo of the FSC (Forest Stewardship Council) use paper taken from forests that have been inspected and certified as meeting the highest standards for environmental and social responsibility. For further information, visit our website at www.cornellpress.cornell.edu.

Cloth printing   10   9   8   7   6   5   4   3   2   1

Paperback printing   10   9   8   7   6   5   4   3   2   1

To my mother,
and to the memory of my father

Contents

List of Illustrations

ix

Preface

xi

Introduction: Colonial Culture

1

1 Colonialism Exposed

21

2 Raymond Roussel and the Structure of Stereotype

47

3 Cannibals in Babylon: René Crevel's Allegories of Exclusion

75

4 A Colonial Princess: Josephine Baker's French Films

97

5 Difference in Disguise: Paul Morand's Black Magic

129

Epilogue: Black-Blanc-Beur

145

Notes

155

References

161

Index

171

Illustrations

1. Workman on the replica of Angkor Wat at the 1931 Exposition coloniale   15
2. Trying on pith helmets at the 1931 Exposition coloniale   22
3. Artisan on display at the 1937 World's Fair   23
4. "Miss France d'Outre-Mer" beauty contestants   38
5. Josephine Baker performing at the Folies Bergère   98
6. Zouzou and Jean as children with Papa Mélé   101
7. Dance number with telephone, *Zouzou*   107
8. Jean's tattoo, *Zouzou*   111
9. Zouzou walking past posters of herself   112
10. Zouzou singing "Haïti"   114
11. Alwina in the ruins of Dougga, *Princesse Tam-Tam*   116
12. Learning to be a lady, *Princesse Tam-Tam*   120
13. The maharajah and Alwina, *Princesse Tam-Tam*   121
14. Alwina enjoying a snack, *Princesse Tam-Tam*   122
15. Poster by Eric Castel, "Three colors, one flag, one empire"   147

Preface

In recent years, there has been an explosion of interest in what is loosely referred to as "postcolonial studies." This fashionable topic has spawned what amounts to an academic industry, with dissertations, books, symposia, and conferences devoted to it. Yet, in the rush to label texts, practices, and discourses "postcolonial," there has been comparatively little consideration of the colonial period. Perhaps this curious and rather glaring omission is a function of postmodernism—there's that prefix again—in which aftereffects are emphasized over sources. Or maybe an era can be fully appreciated, or at least properly scrutinized, only in the harsh light of historical distance: as postmodernism is, perhaps more than anything, a metamodernism, so perhaps postcolonialism is, above all, a metacolonialism, a temporal space in which to take stock of that which precedes it.

When I began this project, around 1990, little work had been done in the field of French colonial studies. To a large extent, the problem was, and still is, that colonialism was not only temporally subsumed in the vague term "postcolonialism"; it was also geographically subsumed in the study of the British empire. To adapt an old political slogan, it is as though all colonialism were postcolonialism, and all empires British. At the same time, the welcome surge of interest in Francophone literatures within French studies has had the ancillary effect of deflecting attention from colonial discourse in metropolitan France, with the result that the images that were disseminated in the *hexagone* at the height of the colonial era have not been given due consideration. Yet an understanding of these images is vital to understanding French culture of the twentieth century, and no doubt of the twenty-first century as well, as French political discourse continues to be dominated by debates surrounding immigration, particularly from former colonies. Now, as in the interwar period, French national identity is defined by France's perception of its place in the world, in relation not only to its geopolitical rivals, such as Germany, Britain, and the United States, but also to the peoples it once colonized.

The French are notoriously slow to come to terms with their past. After all, it was only in 1996 that the army officially recognized the innocence of Captain Alfred Dreyfus, whose wrongful accusation of espionage a century earlier had torn the nation in two. Similarly, it was only in the late 1980s and 1990s, judging by the media attention devoted to the trials of Klaus Barbie and Maurice Papon, that France began coming to terms with its involvement in the Second World War; and, generally speaking, French cultural discourse is still in the repressive stage of what might be called, after Henry Rousso, the Algeria Syndrome (Rousso 1987). At the turn of the twenty-first century, it is the atrocities of its colonial past that France represses, retaining only sanitized memories of the pomp and circumstance, the valor and the glory of France's *mission civilisatrice*. But at the heart of the assimilationist pretensions, or discourse of inclusion, evoked by the buzzword "intégration," there resides a counterdiscourse, a more or less unconscious desire for something different—a desire, in fact, for difference itself, a kind of difference that is grounded in exclusion.

On a personal level, I have not always been prepared for the insistence with which unresolved issues of cultural identity have resurfaced in recent decades. These issues were brought home to me during a chilling experience I had in a Parisian immigration office in 1989, while applying for a *carte de séjour*. I had risen at five in the morning on four occasions, taken a long taxi ride across town, and stood in line in the cold, dark morning for hours, only to be turned away each time for a different bureaucratic reason: the wrong number of photocopies, the incorrect stamp, the wrong-size photographs. On this occasion, I had handed in my passport, received my number, and was standing in the waiting area with perhaps a hundred other people applying to remain in the country, when an official appeared and scanned the faces in the crowd, his eye alighting on a blonde woman, whom he hurried into a cubicle. A minute later, he ushered her back to her place in the line, then caught sight of me and motioned to me to accompany him to one of the cubicles. As I walked in front of the roomful of people who had been waiting even longer than I had, my initial thought, of course, was that I had done something wrong and was going to be deported. When I was seated before the official handling my application, however, she chuckled and explained that, when she had heard there was someone with a U.S. passport among those waiting to be processed, she had sent an assistant out to fetch me in order to speed things up for me, but that he had mistakenly brought back the only other pale-skinned person in the room, a young Polish woman.

I confess that, being at the end of my rope, I did not take the moral high ground at that moment, and sheepishly accepted the dubious privilege being accorded me. It was then, however, that things became truly bizarre. Unable to locate my file from a previous visit to Paris, the woman remarked that such a thing was unusual, especially considering that they still had files going back to the war, stamped "Juif" across the top. Unprompted, she then launched into a tirade about Jews— their ridiculous exaggeration of the events of the war, their disdain of celebrations, their fondness for eating babies—all the while smiling calmly and conspiratorially. I stared at her in wide-eyed, silent disbelief, growing increasingly uncomfortable. Remarkably, she did not seem to pick up on the origin of my own name; it was only later that I realized that this was because the French Bible is based on the Greek translation, which gives "Esdras." The woman cheerfully completed my paperwork and sent me on my way, saying she hoped I enjoyed my time in France.

This extraordinary experience evoked for me several of the different but, I believe, not unrelated issues that I would eventually explore in this book: what I call here the colonial aesthetic, or the transformation of a feature of the body (in this case, skin color) into a sign used to construct a racial hierarchy; the lumping together of individuals designated by this sign into homogeneous groups (dark-skinned, light-skinned) that are opposed to one another *en masse;* France's anxiously ambivalent relationship with other imperial, or, in the case of the United States, culturally imperial, powers; and, finally, the ways in which the arbitrariness of language—a word stamped on a file, a translation from Greek rather than Hebrew—has the potential to produce distinctly nonlinguistic consequences.

Of course, the behavior of a single individual does not in any way paint a representative picture of a nation; nor can the history of French antisemitism be conflated or confused with France's colonial legacy. Nevertheless, it is certainly true that these exclusionary discourses have often gone hand in hand; and both came to a head in the period leading up to the Second World War. But whereas there is a growing body of literature documenting and analyzing antisemitic sentiment in France during this era, little work has been done on assumptions about "race" in the colonial context of the same period. Yet this was precisely the time that colonial rhetoric, and the attendant cult of exoticism, flourished. Both tendencies, racialist and antisemitic, are, at least to some extent, born of the same desire on the part of France to stake out a place for itself in the phantasmatic hierarchy of cultures. It is on the often unconscious desire for such distinctions that assertions of national identity are based.

I must say a word here about my use of psychoanalysis in this book. The term "colonial unconscious" is, to some extent, a heuristic one. Its use should not be taken to imply that I am advancing psychoanalytic principles or methods uncritically as a means of explaining colonial history. I am aware that psychoanalysis—itself a field that has multiple internal divisions and schools of interpretation—is the product of a particular time and place, and that it can often be used to dehistoricize works of art or situations that cannot be fully understood outside their historical context. Moreover, I personally have little patience for literary or cultural analysis that reduces its object to Oedipus this, Oedipus that, or the somewhat puerile game of "Who's got the phallus?" Nevertheless, I am convinced that some basic interpretive models are worth retaining, provided they are used with a certain amount of flexibility and attention to the specific circumstances that have given rise to the text or event being studied. In particular, the psychoanalytic contention that signs are not all that they appear, or, rather, that they are more than they appear (which is, to put it simply, what I mean here by "unconscious"), can provide a fruitful starting point for the study of culture. This interpretive approach, however, should not be confused with a "depth" model, which would imply that by digging far enough below the surface, we could eventually arrive at the "true" meaning of history. What I am suggesting is that colonial discourse, both in the interwar period and in its more recent postcolonial guises, is the product of conflicting desires, desires that, rather than cancel one another out, are mutually reinforcing and, therefore, inseparable.

This book would never have seen the light of day had it not been for the generosity of many people on whom I relied for essential support. I am pleased to have the chance to express my gratitude to them here.

I am very grateful to my colleagues in the University of Stirling French

Department for their encouragement. I especially wish to thank Alison Cooper for all her help, and Siân Reynolds for her many kindnesses.

While working on this project in its initial form, I gained a great deal of advice and support from Anne Berger, Richard Klein, Philip Lewis, and José Piedra, as well as from Kate Bloodgood, who wisely urged patience at all the right times. I would also like to acknowledge here with fond gratitude the lasting influence of some of my undergraduate professors: Norman O. Brown, the late Roberto Crespi, Kristin Ross, Seth Schein, Georges Van Den Abbeele, and Hayden White. I am well aware of my great good fortune in getting to work with these extraordinary teachers.

The chapter on Josephine Baker's films was begun in a National Endowment for the Humanities seminar at the University of Iowa in 1994; that summer was a revelation, introducing me not only to the possibilities of working with film but also to the ongoing inspiration and guidance of the seminar directors, Dudley Andrew and Steve Ungar, to whom I am greatly indebted. I also benefited from interactions with the other seminar participants, particularly Joan Gross, Gregg Siewert, and Florianne Wild.

I wish to thank the following people for their helpful comments on the manuscript at various points in its development: Alastair Duncan, Lynn Laufenberg, Maggie Nolan, and Talia Schaffer. In addition to pointing out some of the weaknesses in my work, these friendly critics offered much-needed encouragement. I am also extremely grateful to Bernhard Kendler at Cornell University Press for his support, which made all the difference.

Throughout the writing of this book, I relied most heavily on two people for suggestions, challenges, and feedback, both in conversation and in the margins of the manuscript. Terry Rowden helped me refine my arguments at every step of the way and provided invaluable intellectual and moral support. Rebecca Spang, too, was immensely helpful, sparking countless ideas. I could not have completed this project without either of these incisive interlocutors.

Needless to say, none of the many people who have provided assistance on this project is implicated in any of the inaccuracies or other intellectual crimes I may have committed here.

Four chapters appeared earlier in slightly different form. I am grateful to their publishers for permission to reprint them here. Part of Chapter 1, "Colonialism Exposed," appeared in *Contemporary French Civilization* 19 (Winter–Spring 1995): 33–49. A second part of the same chapter was published in *Identity Papers: Contested Nationhood in Twentieth-Century France*, edited by Steven Ungar and Tom Conley (Minneapolis: University of Minnesota Press, 1996), reprinted by permission. Part of chapter 2, "Raymond Roussel and the Structure of Stereotype," appeared in *SubStance* #79, vol. 25, no. 1 © 1996, reprinted by permission of the University of Wisconsin Press. Part of Chapter 4, "A Colonial Princess," was published in *French Cultural Studies* 7 (1996): 149–61.

On a personal note, I wish to express my gratitude to Letizia Panizza and Joe Harris in London for lots of good conversation and Christmas pudding; to Beth Ellen Rosenbaum and Al Shapere for their warmhearted encouragement; and to Jennifer Mulcaster and her family in California for their special kindness and support over the years.

Finally, Paul Jackson has shown me the meaning of patience by example. I thank him for enduring this book with me, and me with this book.

Elizabeth Ezra

Edinburgh, Scotland

THE COLONIAL UNCONSCIOUS

Introduction

Colonial Culture

In 1931, the French National Zoological Society held its annual meeting at the Exposition coloniale internationale, in a departure from its traditional venue at the Gare de Lyon. Paul Morand, who presided over the event, summarized the evening's themes in his keynote address:

> I must say that I was a bit disappointed to note the absence of human flesh from this colonial menu. . . . We may not have tasted Man today, but we have eaten animal flesh. This is a compromise solution, replacing human sacrifice, but one that will appear no less abhorrent to our descendants, who will take their nourishment in pill form. When we consume animals, the Blacks say that it is still a divinity that we eat and assimilate. Well, ladies and gentlemen, today we have not only devoured Senegal and the Gambia, we have not only digested Sudan; we have communed with all of Africa [*l'Afrique tout entière*] in the form of a crow and a warthog. (Cited in Capatti 1989, 203)[1]

Morand's remarks may have been broadly rhetorical, but they bespoke a very real phenomenon: the consumption of one culture by another. Between the two world wars, the French public was inundated with images of sub-Saharan Africa, the Maghreb, Southeast Asia, and

1

the West Indies in books, film, advertising, and exhibitions. Above and beyond the merely exotic, which projected images of undifferentiated "otherness," representations of the colonial located cultural difference in specifically political terms, confirming France's military prowess and status as a world power.

Often referred to as the "apogee" or "apotheosis" of French colonialism, the interwar period marks the beginning of the end of a colonial age that had started with the subjugation of Algeria a century earlier. Independence movements were beginning to gain momentum in the colonies, while in the *métropole*, opposition to colonialism mounted: the 1925 Rif War mobilized many left-wing intellectuals, among them Surrealists, in support of the Moroccan rebels; the Algerian independence movement L'Étoile nord-africaine was founded in France in 1926; the nationalist organization Destour, formed in Tunisia in 1920, organized boycotts of French products in the 1930s under the name Néo-Destour; and the Indochinese Communist Party was founded in February 1930 in Hong Kong, in the same year the Yen Bay uprising broke out. Partly in response to these demonstrations of resistance, colonial propaganda efforts in France intensified. According to Raoul Girardet, the interwar years "brought . . . , in contrast to the preceding era, a very noticeable expansion of what can be called the national community's colonial consciousness" (1972, 176). But it was not only official, state-sponsored propaganda that proliferated; what Girardet has called "l'idée coloniale" also began to pervade French culture in contexts that were not officially devoted to colonialism.

My focus in this book is not on French colonization, which is the political and economic domination by one country of others, but rather on French colonialism, or the images of its colonial enterprise that France presented to itself and to the world. In interwar France, these images were everywhere, and they were inescapable. In the decade preceding Morand's postprandial speech, the public had marveled at film footage documenting the exploits of the Citroen-sponsored car races, the Croisières noire and jaune; the public could read about the ethnographic Mission Dakar-Djibouti (the spoils of which would be displayed in the Musée de l'homme, inaugurated in 1937) in Michel Leiris's highly personal *Afrique fantôme*; they could also read André Gide's account of colonial rule in *Le Voyage au Congo*, or they could watch the documentary film by the same name made by Gide's friend Marc Allégret (who would go on to direct Josephine Baker in the box-office success *Zouzou*). A fascination with things colonial also bolstered the popularity of the missionary Père Foucauld, spawning the controversial cinematic homage to Foucauld's *mission civilisatrice* in the 1936 *Appel du silence*. In literature, Blaise Cendrars's *Anthologie nègre* found a large audience in 1921, and in the same year, René Maran's *Batouala* provoked a maelstrom of outrage when it was awarded the Prix Goncourt, the first such prize to go to an author of African ancestry. Also that year, Jacques Feyder's enormously popular *L'Atlantide* (the highest-grossing French film of the 1920s), based on Pierre Benoit's 1919 best-selling novel, would launch the vogue for *cinéma colonial* that would fill theaters through the next decade. At the beginning of the 1930s, Céline's depiction of colonial Africa in *Voyage au bout de la nuit*, published the year after the lavish celebrations to comemorate the centennial of the conquest of Algeria, coincided with the first stirrings of Negritude (given voice in journals such as *L'Étudiant noir* and *Légitime défense*). Throughout the 1930s, a growing emphasis was placed on colonial issues in mass-circulation papers such as *L'Echo de Paris*, *Le Petit Parisien*, and *Le Figaro;* special supplements and even entire issues devoted to the empire were published by *Le Temps*, *Les Annales*, and *l'Illustration* (see Montagnon 1988, 458). Meanwhile, children thrilled to the adventures of Tintin, whose exploits often took him to French colonial possessions, and of Babar the elephant, a native of Africa who sometimes ventured out of his colonial homeland, and people of all ages breakfasted on Banania drink powder, whose box featured the grinning "Y'a bon" Senegalese soldier. And throughout the *entre-deux-guerres*, people flocked to the colonial exhibitions, grandiose tributes to France's imperial might, from the 1922 national exhibition held in Marseille to the colonial section of the 1937 World's Fair. Among this series of exhibitions, the crown jewel was the 1931 Exposition coloniale internationale, which influenced a generation of writers and artists such as Antonin Artaud, whose experience watching the Balinese dancers moved him to create his *théâtre de la cruauté*, and the composer Olivier Messaien, on whose music the exhibition was to have a lasting effect.[2]

So, in a sense, Morand's remarks at the Exposition coloniale rang true. French culture had indeed devoured colonial culture, making it an integral part of itself. Morand's speech provided the perfect emblem of *la plus grande France*, assimilating entire continents ("l'Afrique tout entière," for example) in a single bite. Colonial rhetoric touted the universalist merits of this Greater France (or Greatest, depending on one's grammatical—and historical—perspective) composed of the "100 million Frenchmen," according to the often-invoked phrase, who made up France's colonial empire and to whom centralized primary schooling taught French cultural values. This was a France greater than the *hexagone*, but also greater than its geopolitical rivals—such as Britain, whose imperial prowess overshadowed France's; the United States, whose emerging world hegemony was at once disseminated by and reflected in its culture industry; and Germany, the military rival that would give meaning to the expression "interwar period." Not only was *la plus grande France* greater than its rivals, it was also the greatest France that had ever been, greater even than itself, surpassing its pre-Napoleonic colonial holdings several fold. This, then, was what Herman Lebovics (1994) has called "True France," France's greatest self, its greatest moment, made possible by its overseas mirror image, *la France d'Outre-Mer*. But was this overseas France a part of greater France, or was it a separate France? Was it considered capable of attaining Frenchness at all? Or was there something about Frenchness that transcended the acquisition of nationality and language, lying beyond the grasp of those not born with it?

Some colonial administrators and theorists argued that there was. At the turn of the twentieth century, the doctrine of association challenged assimilationist policies, which sought to transform colonial possessions into miniatures of France.[3] Implemented by Hubert Lyautey in the "pacification" of Morocco shortly after the turn of the century, association emphasized the cultural distinctiveness of each colonial possession, its unassimilability to the *métropole*. Association claimed to respect indigenous customs; it was presented, according to Martin Deming Lewis, as "a kind of partnership of the colonial peoples with the metropolitan power, for mutual benefit" (Lewis 1962, 150). Association, as it was promoted, would have amounted to a recognition of the cultural, if not political, autonomy of the countries under colonial rule. The goal of assimilation, in contrast, inspired by the egalitarian rhetoric of the French Revolution, was to make model French citizens of colonial subjects, who were taught the intricacies of French language and culture in a centralized educational system. The ensuing strategic debate pointed up the complexity of the relationship between identity and difference in colonial discourse.

In both cases, however, the distance between rhetoric and reality was great. In most colonial possessions, there were separate governing bodies for indigenous people and French colonists. Citizenship was granted only in the "anciennes colonies" (former colonies)—the Antilles, Guyana, Réunion Island, and the four "communes" of Senegal—and even then, it was often far from automatic.[4] A case in point is West Africa, of which Michael Crowder has said that "the African had no policy-making role, not even at the level of local government as the chief had in the Native Authority system in British West Africa. . . . Only if he managed to gain a good French education, become Christian, and prove his loyalty to France through service could he become 'assimilated' and gain the rights of a French citizen. Before 1945 less than five hundred Africans had become assimilated in this way" (Crowder 1969, 62). The hypocrisy of a policy that barred access to the very equality it preached was underscored by Albert Memmi in 1957: "The colonialist never planned to transform the colony into the image of his homeland, or to re-make the colonized in his own image! He cannot allow such an equa-tion—it would destroy the principle of his privileges" (1970, 69).

A striking example of the ambivalence of colonial rhetoric can be seen in a promotional statement written in 1937 by Henry Béranger, who served the empire in a triple capacity as senator of Guadeloupe, presi-dent of the Commission des Affaires étrangères of the French Senate, and president of the Commission de la France d'Outre-Mer at the world's fair. Béranger begins his preface to *L'Empire colonial français à l'Ile des Cygnes* by emphasizing the cohesion between colony and *métropole*: "Overseas provinces, our possessions on the five continents, complete, by a natural extension, the artistic and technological tableau of our na-tive provinces" (Béranger 1937, 5). Yet only three paragraphs after hav-ing asserted this assimilationist view of the colonies as an extension of France, Béranger suggests the opposite view by using the word "associ-ation," which, although in this context it applies to the relationship be-tween France and other world powers, necessarily evokes the connota-tion specific to early twentieth-century colonial discourse: "In the light of modern evolution, which has impelled so many great nations to be no longer the provinces of a given continent, but instead, veritable intercon-tinental systems reaching across the globe, France has staked out its place as the creator of an ideal comprising an association of races [*un idéal d'association des races*]" (5). The word "province" changes meaning from one paragraph to the next: the overseas "provinces" would enable France to outgrow the boundaries that would otherwise limit its status to that of a European province. By effacing differences between the *métropole* and the colonies, "*la plus grande France*" would be able to dif-ferentiate itself from the rest of Europe. The altered meaning ascribed to the word "province" in the second quotation also makes it necessary to take the word "association" to refer to cultural *assimilation*, a concept to which it would normally be opposed in colonial discourse. The ambigu-ity of the phrase "idéal d'association des races," which can refer either to relations between France and its colonies or to relations between France and other world powers, results in the seemingly contradictory assertions of the colonies as both assimilated and associated, at once a part of and separate from France. Colonial administrators were unable to choose between asserting the assimilability of the colonial possessions and proclaiming their irreducible alterity because they needed to do both: the politics of inclusion, which appealed to nationalist concerns about military strength, was inseparable from the politics of exclusion, which appealed to xenophobic impulses.

The apparently opposing doctrines of assimilation and association could be summarized in a question: Were the colonies so different that they could not be made French, or were they destined to validate France's universalist pretensions, which date back to the Enlightenment? The dichotomy implicit in this question, of course, is a false one. Assimilation and association were two sides of a single coin: both fell prey to the same fundamental contradiction and were thus equally impossible in practice. Association assumed a partnership among equals that did not exist, because the relationship between France and its colonies was based not on equality but rather on political and cultural domination. Like that of assimilation, the notion of association glossed over the contradiction inherent in the notion of a partnership between colonizer and colonized. As Georges Balandier has noted, "The colonial relationship is by definition inauthentic; it cannot at once institute domination and recognize the Other" (Balandier 1984, 3). Although both assimilation and association were integral components of colonial rhetoric, the context of subjugation that gave rise to them precluded their enactment in practice. One official in the ministry for the colonies called the alternatives "unrealisable assimilation or hypocritical association, two systems in equally flagrant contradiction of the facts" (Suret-Canale 1971, 85). Each discourse merely reflected a different form of spin control, a different way of serving up colonialism to the general public.[5] The tension between these discourses exemplifies Fredric Jameson's observation in *The Political Unconscious* that "within the symbolic power of art and culture the will to dominate perseveres intact" (Jameson 1981, 299). It is this will to dominate, more than anything else, that characterizes the colonial unconscious.

Although assimilation was predicated on the eventual eradication of distinctions among groups, the disappearance of these distinctions was implicitly feared and rejected. In the works studied here, which serve as prime examples of colonial wish fulfillment, assimilation is repeatedly shown to be impossible, invariably thwarted by some "essential" difference, no matter how small, that remains. The possibility of assimilation was precluded by the combined imposition and denial of distinctions: colonial discourse imposed distinctions between colonizers and colonized, while denying distinctions among the colonized. French cultural texts reiterated this paradox: on the one hand, there was much talk of assimilation, but on the other, there was much talk about the supposedly inherent differences between colonizers and colonized. As cultures were brought together through commerce, colonial settlement, and immigration, their differences from one another were magnified, while differences among members of the dominated culture were minimized or denied altogether.

The function of identifying logic in colonialism has been noted by Abdul JanMohamed, who analyzes the process by which group identities are constructed:

> The European writer commodifies the native by negating his individuality, his subjectivity, so that he is now perceived as a generic being that can be exchanged for any other native (they all look alike, act alike, and so on). Once reduced to his exchange-value in the colonialist signifying system, he is fed into the manichean allegory, which functions as the currency, the medium of exchange for the entire colonialist discursive system. (1986, 83)

If extended beyond the limits of "colonialist fiction" to which he confines it, JanMohamed's theory of human exchange value becomes a useful tool for analyzing colonial rhetoric in its broader cultural context.

It is important at this point to stress that assimilation in the colonial context remained an abstraction not because of "race," whose very existence has often been questioned, but because of racism, whose existence was (and continues to be) all too prevalent.[6] The promotion of assimilation thus resulted in what Homi Bhabha has called colonial mimicry, or "a desire for a reformed, recognizable Other, as *a subject of difference that is almost the same, but not quite*. Which is to say, that the discourse of mimicry is constructed around an *ambivalence*; in order to be effective, mimicry must continually produce its slippage, its excess, its difference" (Bhabha 1994, 318). Unlike Bhabha, however, I do not believe that colonial ambivalence represents "potentially and strategically an insurgent counter-appeal" (91) which, as Bhabha argues in another essay, "enables a form of subversion, founded on the undecidability that turns the discursive conditions of dominance into the grounds of intervention" (112).

Quite the opposite: far from "disrupt[ing] its authority" (88), the double-ness of French colonial discourse reinforces it, providing a sort of reverse *doublure*, or lining, that protects it from the outside—a wolf in sheep's clothing. For in fact, colonial ambivalence neither enabled resistance nor prevented it. The French empire did not self-destruct; it was over-thrown. And it was not overthrown by colonial ambivalence. It seems an (unconsciously) imperialist gesture to locate the possibility of subver-sion within colonial discourse itself: this is to colonize resistance, to ap-propriate it for the colonizers, thereby denying an active role to those who actually do the resisting.

This book, however, is not about resistance; it is about the discursive structures that persisted throughout and beyond the colonial era, and whose durability can be attributed to the fact that they say one thing and do another. All the works I discuss would seem to celebrate the mixing of cultures, but they actually seek to preserve the exotic as such—that is, to keep it literally outside (*ex*). This ambivalence is expressed in various ways: it informs Morand's *négrophilie;* Crevel's alternation between cele-bration and condemnation of the noble savage myth; Roussel's simulta-neous engagement in and deconstruction of racial stereotyping; the rap-prochement and ultimate separation of spectators and human exhibits at the colonial exhibitions (as well as the opposite movement, namely the domestication of a too-threatening difference); and the combination of adoration and domination projected onto Josephine Baker in her French films. All these cultural texts reveal the double bind of a discourse that precludes the possibility of the very assimilation it invites; they all ex-ploit the ambivalence that characterizes the French colonial experience.

It is worth noting here that the *degree* of ambivalence may differ from one work to the next and that it might well be possible to differentiate among levels of perniciousness of the images used (placing, for example, Morand, with his overtly racist beliefs, at one end of the spectrum and Crevel, with his well-intentioned if flawed anticolonialist credentials, at the other). Nevertheless, I have tried to maintain a relatively analytical stance when discussing these works, because it would be all too easy to individualize blame for a widespread problem, thus obviating any fur-ther need to contend with a more general cultural phenomenon. The ex-tent to which we can speak of a colonial "discourse" at all, however heuristically, reflects the extent to which that discourse extends beyond both individuals and intentions. Consequently, the choice of literary and cinematic texts examined in this book was determined precisely by the fact that they were not explicitly "colonial"; with the exception of the colonial exhibitions, which were official expressions of colonial propaganda, the texts and cultural products studied here had no special institutional affiliation with colonialism.

The juxtaposition of the works of these authors with accounts of the colonial exhibitions is perhaps not a self-evident one. None of the writers or filmmakers studied here is known as a "colonial" writer (and it is not my intention to argue otherwise). Colonialism does not even figure prominently as a theme in the particular literary and filmic texts I examine. Yet this is precisely the reason these works interest me: I wanted to see to what extent colonial ideology was "in the air," to what extent it had made an impact on both explicit propaganda and the work of artists for whom colonialism was not a central concern. I have juxtaposed the official with the unofficial in order to illustrate the ubiquity of what Raoul Girardet has called "l'idée coloniale," the idea of the colonial, and the extent to which it pervaded cultural life in a variety of contexts. The themes and rhetoric that pervade the colonial exhibitions find a less self-conscious, but equally forceful, expression in the surrounding culture: these less explicit manifestations of colonial discourse, I argue, indicate the presence of a "colonial unconscious," the mechanisms of which are best examined in works whose colonial content has tended to go unnoticed. It is for this reason that, instead of studying the *roman colonial*, which placed adventurous French protagonists in a dangerous and exotic colonial empire, I discuss the work of authors not known primarily for their positions on colonialism, whose colonial settings or characters are incidental to the plot, a small and seemingly insignificant detail that evokes large and significant truths about the *idée coloniale* in France. Similarly, I have bypassed the *cinéma colonial*, so popular in the 1930s, to examine instead films that play on the exotic but whose main objective is not the portrayal of life in the colonies. The films studied here were star vehicles for Josephine Baker, whose status as an African-American in Paris situated her at the crossroads of competing cultural imperialisms.

Colonial culture is so ubiquitous, so visible, as to be nearly imperceptible. It is both celebratory and mundane. It is the domestication of the exotic, and the defamiliarization of the familiar; it is a simultaneous attraction to and repulsion of difference. But above all, it is ambivalent. It follows, then, that this ambivalence pervades those epistemological traditions whose development has been coextensive with that of colonial expansion: Africanist and Orientalist discourses. Africanist discourse, according to Christopher Miller, is divided between "favorable and unfavorable" utterances (1985, 249), between attraction and repulsion, between the noble savage and the frightening cannibal. Unlike Orientalism's systematizing representational mode, Africanist discourse resists the desire for rational explanation even as it seeks it; it searches, and insists on finding "nothing." Orientalism, in contrast, is a product and expression of the desire to reduce its objects to a knowable, quantifiable field of study and classification (Said 1979).

In the context of French colonialism, the terms "Orientalism" and "Africanist discourse" exceed their geographical referents. Although France's colonial empire extended all over the globe, colonial culture was dominated by these two rhetorical positions, which at once illuminated and obscured their objects. In the twentieth century, France's possessions on the African continent dominated the public consciousness, a domination made greater still during the Algerian War. It is perhaps not surprising, then, that the Maghreb became the focus of such intense desire and loathing in the twentieth century, from its prolific representation in film and literature, to the immigration debate that continues to shape France's political landscape. North Africa, especially, is seen to lie at the crossroads of these two discourses, in terms of both location and rhetoric; alternately Oriental or African, often both, the region has long been the object of conflicting ambitions. But then, images of the Maghreb are only the most complete expressions of French colonial ambivalence in general. French colonialism exploits this tension between the desire to know everything and the desire not to know, or the desire to know nothing.

Colonial rhetoric places particular emphasis on projecting into the present a past that was quickly becoming obsolete, as the colonial empire began to dissolve. In this sense, the products of colonial culture— the exhibitions, books, films, and so on—were what Pierre Nora has called *lieux de mémoire*, whose "fundamental purpose," he says, "is to stop time, to inhibit forgetting, to fix a state of things" (1996, 15). But at the same time that they erected "lieux de mémoire," I would argue, these cultural manifestations expressed a collective desire to forget. The synthesis of these conflicting commemorative agendas results in a special kind of knowledge that rests on ignorance. This ignorance is forced, the product of a repression that submerges the atrocities wrought by colonial domination in the depths of a cultural unconscious. This desire to know nothing perhaps offers a way of understanding the tensions that define the relationship between France and its former colonies and that foreclose the possibility of assimilation for postcolonial immigrants. In "Sujets ou citoyens?" Étienne Balibar writes:

Thus the notion of "cultural proximity" that informs debates about immigration—a notion that is indissociable, explicitly or implicitly, from that of assimilation . . . —is entirely a product of colonization. It has meaning only in a retrospective comparison: European immigrants from before the Second World War or today are said to be "close" because they came or come from countries that are "equal," because they were never colonized by France, unlike North Africans, blacks, and Asians. (1984, 1741)

The notion of cultural proximity not only accounts for the special predicament of immigrants who come from formerly colonized countries; it also sheds light on colonial discourse in the period studied here. The alien status attributed to the former colonies results from their prior contact with France: paradoxically, it is their familiarity that makes them seem distant. The cultural separatism seemingly based on difference or strangeness thus masks the fact that it is really based on excessive familiarity. The French "know" the formerly colonized in a way they do not know those they did not colonize; and the repression of this familiarity transforms it into its opposite, strangeness: Freud's *Unheimlich* (uncanny).

Freud describes the *Unheimlich* as "in reality nothing new or alien, but something which is familiar and old-established in the mind and which has become alienated from it only through the process of repression" (Freud 1981, 17:241). The uncanny, then, describes the recognition of something in the world that resembles, repeats, or evokes something that has been repressed in the psyche: it is the return of the repressed from the outside. The terrible familiarity wrought by colonization is hidden beneath the disguise of the alien. Repressing (in the psychoanalytic sense) colonial repression (in the political sense) causes the too-familiar to seem too different. Even where difference appears to be hidden (as in Morand's tales of *almost* imperceptible differences revealed, and the minimal difference that always thwarts efforts to assimilate in Roussel's plays), it is the agent of a double masking: the gesture of "exposing" hidden differences merely obscures further a terrifying familiarity. In these cases, it is not the mask, but rather the unmasking, that conceals.

In *Strangers to Ourselves*, Julia Kristeva argues that the impression of foreignness results when one projects one's own feelings of ambivalence about oneself onto others. Rather than serve as an external source of anxiety, "foreigners" serve to trigger an anxiety that stems from within. The key to overcoming this feeling of strangeness, Kristeva contends, resides in the recognition or knowledge of this repression (which reverses the repression of the knowledge): "How could one tolerate a foreigner if one did not know one was a stranger to oneself?" (1991, 182). Somewhat optimistically, she attributes to psychoanalysis the power to solve problems caused by racial divisions and nationalist conflicts. Freud, she says, "teaches us how to detect foreignness in ourselves. That is perhaps the only way not to hound it outside of us" (1991, 191). The fact remains, however, that many French have less trouble "tolerating" Norwegians, Japanese, or Australians than they do North Africans: and this prejudicial hierarchy is the product of France's colonial history.

In the interwar period, this history was articulated using the language of "race." An example of such language can be found in a summary of France's goals for its immigration policy in 1920, which was designed "to appeal to a workforce of European origin rather than a colonial or exotic workforce, because of the difficulties of a social or ethnic order that might result from the presence on French soil of ethnographic elements that are too clearly distinct from the rest of the population" (Laurent Bonnevay, cited in Bonnet 1976, 121). This statement reminds us that the concept of racial difference is often expressed through metaphors of visual perception. Yet even when it is not an explicitly visual trope, the abstract concept of assimilation based on contractual equality fades in the shadow of the apparently essential determinates of race, determinates that can be found in every one of the texts studied here. The discovery of these determinates, however, is not given as automatic: they must be carefully exposed in an elaborate ritual of unmasking, in which difference, depicted as disguised or hidden, is brought to light.

The rhetoric of exposure assumed its most fully articulated form at the colonial exhibitions, whose function was literally to expose (*exposition*) colonialism to the French—and to monied tourists from all over the world. As John M. MacKenzie eloquently puts it, "The exhibitions sucked the world into patterns of dependence, dominance and subjection on one great site" (cited by Greenhalgh 1988, x). In the same way that (and perhaps because) a colonial exhibition was meant to be a condensed version of the French colonial empire, it concentrated the central themes of colonial rhetoric, which had been developing for centuries, in the context of a single cultural event. Between the two world wars, the French government poured enormous amounts of money and time into creating the appearance of a prospering, humanitarian colonial empire. Nowhere is this effort more visible than at the 1931 Exposition coloniale internationale (ECI) and the colonial section of the 1937 Exposition internationale des arts et techniques, or world's fair, both held in Paris. These were the major French-sponsored international exhibitions between the world wars that were devoted entirely or in part to representing the French colonial empire. They can be seen, in retrospect, as manifestations of French imperialism's last gasp.

Chapter 1, "Colonialism Exposed," focuses primarily on media representations of the human exhibits—people brought from the colonies and displayed zoolike in their "natural" environment, or architectural simulations thereof, in order to add "authenticity" and exotic flavor to the exhibitions. In the sections of this book called "exhibits," I discuss the ways in which the people who were subjected to colonial domination were represented by the creators of colonial rhetoric. In these sections, I do not concentrate on the publications intended for a specific audience personally involved in colonialism (although I refer occasionally to such publications). Rather, my focus is on non-novelistic narratives intended for a general audience. These include pamphlets, brochures, and guidebooks published by exhibition organizers for exhibition visitors, as well as newspaper and magazine articles printed in the mainstream press and in publications sponsored by political parties.

The 1931 exhibition, organized by the marshal Hubert Lyautey, who had championed the "associationist" system of indirect rule and the creation of Morocco's protectorate status, emphasized the cultural differences between France and its colonial possessions. But it was equally anxious to demonstrate the extent to which the colonies had benefited from France's presence. The exhibition succeeded in projecting far and wide the image of France as a civilizing force in the world, as we can see in the article "Cannibals Will Show Progress," which appeared in the March 17, 1931, *El Paso Herald*:

> A typical "cannibal village," populated by natives whose grandfathers were authentic cannibals, will be one of the picturesque features of the International Colonial Exposition. . . .
>
> For purposes of contrast, there will be two villages showing the natives "before and after" exposure to French colonial methods.
>
> "Before" will visualize a Pahouin village near Libresville [*sic*], as it existed about half a century ago. No sanitation; no school house; the most primitive barbarism.
>
> "After" will reveal a pahouin [*sic*] village today, with a school house, European standards of sanitation, and everybody attired in colonial fashion, in spotless white.

The Albany (N.Y.) *News* of March 12, 1931, and the Kenosha (Wis.) *News* of March 27 print the same article word for word, with the following addition: "These Pahouins of today wear horn-rim glasses and some of them write their letters on a typewriter. They have adopted many European ideas and ideals, and they have abandoned cannibalism forever."

The "before and after" model has always held a privileged place in colonial discourse. Routinely adopted as a means of justifying colonial domination, this paradigm is invoked constantly in French accounts of the 1931 exhibition. The theme is typically formulated as "the rapid transformation of peoples who would have remained in the most wretched state of barbarism without the intervention of the great colonial states" (Vivier de Streel 1932, 8). Colonization even bestows history where there is none: "A small community without history until the French occupation of Morocco, Fedhala was, for a long time, no more than a point on the map" (Nicoll 1931, 171).

The most visible icon of progress at the 1931 ECI, a full-scale reproduction of Angkor Wat, the great Khmer temple, was actually nothing new. Replicas of the Angkor Wat had been drawing visitors to world and colonial exhibitions since the nineteenth century (see Norindr 1996). The temple became an overdetermined symbol of France's colonial prowess, boasting the conquest of a culture that had once been wealthy and powerful enough to produce a monument of unequaled grandeur— and serving as a reminder of the source of skilled labor capable of producing such grandeur again, only this time in the service of French interests. But above all, Angkor Wat symbolized the benevolent influence bestowed by France on its colonial empire. One commentator draws a parallel between the upward sweep of French colonial "progress" and the building's majestic exterior stairway, which apparently went up but not down: "All the measurable forms of intellectual and material progress advance [*s'élèvent*] step by step with all the symbolic force of the powerful staircase leading up the great temples of Angkor" (Louis Forest in *Le Matin*, July 24, 1922, cited in Artaud 1924, 534). The French appeared to be responsible not only for the material and intellectual progress the temple represented but also for the temple itself: "Has one of the benefits of our Indochinese colonization not been to return to a great but forgetful people this temple of Angkor, dazzling testament to an ancient splendor? Let us not forget that it was the naturalist Mouhout who, during a voyage of exploration in 1861, discovered the temple of Angkor, buried for four centuries" (*Ce qu'il faut voir* 1931, 52). Implicit in this statement is the suggestion that, were it not for France's interven-

Figure 1. *A workman puts the finishing touches on the replica of Angkor Wat at the 1931 Exposition coloniale. Sygma/Keystone.*

tion, Khmer culture would be lost forever. Here the colonizer is the restorer of History, a restoration imposed as the necessary prerequisite to the attainment of Progress.

The myth of progress, of course, is not specific to any given form of colonialism. What distinguished French colonial rhetoric of the interwar period was its self-referential invocation of the myth, which suggested that France was trying to make peace with its own past. In the opening article of the special issue of *L'Illustration* devoted to the ECI, Lyautey takes care to distinguish the 1931 exhibition from the 1915 Exposition de Casablanca, which he had also organized: "But the Exhibition of Casablanca was, on the whole, nothing but a war machine. Yesterday, we inaugurated a great work of peace" (*L'Illustration*, May 23, 1931, un-paginated). The concern to differentiate between the ECI and its precursors is indicative of a larger attempt to convey the image of a new and improved imperialism. This concern can be detected in the confessional tone of another article in the same issue of *L'Illustration*, "L'Exposition coloniale oeuvre de Paix." The author, the Gouverneur général Olivier, Lyautey's collaborator, writes that colonization "was the strength and the pride of Western nations, which did sometimes get so carried away by this pride that they abused their strength, but even schoolchildren know that nations, like men, are subject to error, and that with nations, as with men, wisdom is more often than not the result of a long series of mistakes. Colonization has righted its wrongs. The face that it is showing at Vincennes has peaceful features."

The implication was that both colonizer and colonized had progressed as a result of prolonged contact with one another. The notion of progress would again be emphasized at the 1937 World's Fair—but in what seemed to be very different terms. Whereas the ECI, under Lyautey's guiding hand, had highlighted the benefits to be gained from preserving the cultural boundaries separating colonizers from colonized, the 1937 world's fair appeared to stress the assimilationist potential of the colonized. This emphasis on assimilation was especially visible in the "Miss France d'Outre-Mer" (Miss Overseas France) contest, a beauty pageant whose participants were the offspring of unions between French men and women from the colonies. Despite the assimilationist rhetoric, however, the privileging of racial difference ultimately undercut the contest's integrationist claims. The contest, called "The Best Colonial Marriage" competition and billed as a "living demonstration of eugenics," merged colonial discourse with the pseudobiological theories of racial engineering that were gaining ascendancy as France tried both to emulate and to define itself in opposition to German social policy.

The colonial exhibitions demonstrated to the French public how fruitfully colonial labor—in both the productive and the reproductive senses—could be appropriated for French needs. By displaying the uses to which colonials could be put, the exhibitions confirmed the "mise en valeur" of the colonies in an age when their profitability was often questioned. The exhibitions previewed, and thus facilitated, the transition from a colonial to a third-world economy, from the exploitation of raw materials to that of human labor. Both the image of colonials at work and that of the exotic women of childbearing age bolstered France's status as a world power: in the first instance, as an industrial power with a large work force, and in the second instance, as a military giant capable of producing an army from among its colonial subjects that could compete with those of its rivals.

In both instances, however, and despite the claims being made, the explicit aims of assimilation were undermined. Journalistic accounts of the exhibitions emphasized the strict division that was constructed between the colonizer and colonized, subject and object of the imperial gaze. This boundary, constitutive of colonial identities, was predicated on the dissolution of boundaries within the groups that stood on either side of it. What is sacrificed in colonial discourse, as in any systematized opposition, are the differences among "those" people grouped together in a mass that is opposed to "these" people grouped together: heterogeneity among individuals *within* groups is thus transformed into heterogeneity or difference *between* groups. The classifying discourse that revokes heterogeneity among individuals in order to invoke it between groups is what I refer to as the identification of difference. By identification, I mean two seemingly opposed functions that are actually inseparable: on the one hand, the criterion of sameness used to group together individuals into a single mass; and, on the other hand, the criterion of difference used to distinguish one group from another.

The substitution of difference between groups for differences among individuals results in an implied substitutability of one person for another. It is this transitive logic that enables sacrifice, which hinges on the idea of minimal but essential difference: minimal, in that members of the "sacrificeable category" are encouraged to assimilate into the community, but essential in that they are always doomed to fail. René Girard writes, "The victim must be neither too familiar to the community nor too foreign to it" (1977, 271). This sacrificial difference—almost a form of Bhabha's colonial ambivalence, but not quite—is operative in all the products of colonial culture, but it plays an especially important role in the two plays Raymond Roussel wrote in the interwar period. In *L'Étoile au front*, sacrifice is thematized explicitly, as a pair of twin girls from French colonial India are kidnapped and threatened with immolation if their protector, a half-French, half-Indian woman, does not agree to marry the kidnapper. The function of sacrifice—which eliminates an individual in order to preserve a group—mirrors the identification of difference, in which difference among individuals is eliminated only to be resurrected among groups. This interplay between identity and difference is emblematized in the recurring figures of the twins (represented by the Indian girls) and the métis(se) (at once feminine—the French-Indian woman—and masculine—the part-divine, part-human Christ, who appears in one of the play's anecdotes and, implicitly, in Girard's work on sacrifice). The figure of the twins represents the interchangeability of individuals; and the figure of the métis(se), like the "Miss France d'Outre-Mer" contestants, appears to efface differences while actually evoking two distinct groups represented by each of its halves.

The identification of difference acquires a temporal dimension in Roussel's *Poussière de soleils*, as the division between "us" and "them" coincides with that between "now" and "then." Modernity is defined in opposition to the primitive, which is perceived as a static temporality, eternally self-present and unmarked by change. This lack of differentiation is precisely what differentiates the primitive from the modern. This distinction, and the discourse of discovery that it underwrites, also inform the three human sciences that came of age in the early twentieth century: anthropology (in which the primitive is located "over there," in some distant land), historiography (in which the primitive is located "back then," in some distant time), and psychoanalysis (in which the primitive lies in the recesses of each individual's past). The discourse of discovery is above all a mode of self-recognition, which reinforces the discoverers' sense of their own ethnic, social, or personal superiority. The images of colonialism disseminated in literature, film, and popular exhibitions, while purporting to offer (to borrow Memmi's terms) so many *portraits du colonisé*, actually present a more accurate *portrait du colonisateur*.

The idea of the primitive thus serves above all to legitimate exclusionary practices. Primitives are located outside civilized society, deemed radically different from those inside and indistinguishable from one another. The lack of differentiation constitutive of absolute difference is often allegorized in the image of the cannibal, whose failure to observe boundaries among individuals, through the literal absorption of others, sets the *anthropophage* apart from the rest of "us." In René Crevel's 1927 novel *Babylone*, the image of the cannibal embodies the distinction between inside and outside that is central to the construction of collective identity—and to the exclusionary practices authorized by stereotype. In psychoanalysis, cannibalism is accorded a privileged place in both ontogenetic development (as in Klein's "cannibalistic stage," a child's projection of its devouring impulse onto others) and phylogenetic evolution (as in Freud's controversial account of the origins of civilization in *Totem and Taboo*). An incidence of cannibalism, believed by Freud to have actually taken place, lives on in civilization's collective memory, associated unconsciously with the incest prohibition; both prohibitions are crucial to the establishment of a dichotomy between the civilized and the uncivilized. As a sign of savagery, cannibalism—a bodily act that ignores the distinction among bodies—is linked in Crevel's novel to nudity, another highly coded stereotype of the uncivilized, which transforms the body into a sign.

While Crevel set about depicting the distinctions between civilized and uncivilized consumption, the French culture industry was busy presenting Josephine Baker, the music-hall sensation and sometime film star, as the uncivilized object of civilized cultural consumption. Baker, an American, was herself a popular French icon, who at once symbolized and reinforced France's rivalry with three world powers: Britain, Germany, and the United States. First, her very presence in France served as a reminder of the assimilationist pretension that differentiated France's colonial empire from the British empire's noncentralized, associationist style of colonial rule. Second, the colonials included in France's assimilationist embrace greatly increased France's military manpower and, like the *tirailleurs sénégalais* who had fought in the First World War, would bolster its position in any future conflict with Germany. Finally, Baker's success in France challenged the hegemony of American cultural imperialism: initially rejected by her native country, Baker made French films and sang French songs, which were accessible to Americans only by importation; moreover, here was an American, representative of the cultural imperialism that was coming to dominate France, cast in films that portrayed her as a subject of the French *mission civilisatrice*. The bulk of Baker's film career is represented in *Zouzou* (1934) and *Princesse Tam-Tam* (1935), star vehicles made to cash in on her status as a music-hall legend. Both films construct an image of French national identity by depicting characters who fail to assimilate into the dominant culture. In an era of mounting xenophobia, these works thematized the exclusionary rhetoric invoked to hold together a society on the verge of collapse. Each film expresses colonial ambivalence, taking its protagonist, played by Baker, to the threshold of acceptance in French cultural life before ultimately deeming her foreignness to be insurmountable. This ambivalence was echoed in a telling moment of cultural confusion when Baker was named Queen of the Colonies at the 1931 Exposition coloniale, despite the protests of spoilsports who pointed out that the United States could not technically be considered a French colony.

The differences that prevent Baker's characters from integrating fully into French society also drive Paul Morand's tales of failed assimilation in *Magie noire* (1928), which played an influential role in the negrophilia vogue of the period. The stories studied here depict the thwarted efforts of people with African ancestry to "pass" for white: in "Adieu New York," an African-American woman is forced to return to Africa, where she discovers her "true" identity; in "Excelsior," a light-skinned African-American is ostracized when her skin mysteriously turns black. In his stories as well as in the theories on race advanced in his essays, Morand relied heavily on what anthropologist James Clifford has called the ethnographic allegory of salvage, which attempts to preserve disappearing cultural differences by capturing them in discourse. But rather than posit these differences as proof of an underlying common humanity, which was the goal of contemporary ethnographers, Morand suggested that such (in his view, essential) differences demonstrated an inherent inequality among races. The fact that Morand, known for his extensive world travels and cosmopolitan lifestyle, could be such a strong proponent of ethnic separatism reflects synecdochically the contradiction that pervaded the entire era: although the interwar period in France is often identified with a love of the exotic (the Jazz Age) and assimilationist rhetoric, time and again its cultural representations emphasized (or invented) difference, denying the very possibility of assimilation.

This problematic continues today. The immigration debate in France revolves around the ambiguous and fraught expression "droit à la différence," an idea with leftist origins that has been newly appropriated by the New Right, whose ideologues urge the repatriation of immigrants. Controversies such as the *affaire du foulard* (in which Muslim girls were banned from wearing their head scarves at a state-run school), which resonated throughout the 1990s, suggest that the relationship between French national identity and cultural difference has reemerged with as much relevance in recent times as in the period between the world wars. This relevance is underscored by the rhetoric used to celebrate France's victory in the 1998 World Cup—examined in the epilogue—which bears an uncanny resemblance to colonial discourse of the interwar period. Étienne Balibar points out that the term "postcolonial era" is misleading, suggesting as it does that France has "moved on" from its colonial experience: "Actually, the opposite is true, to a large extent: contemporary France was formed in and through colonization" (1984, 1741). Contemporary French culture, in other words, cannot be understood without an examination of the unconscious colonial legacy that gave rise to it.

꽃

Colonialism Exposed

Laissez mappemondes, cartes et atlas. Partez pour la Porte d'Orée. Le rêve est complaisant. . . . La Grande France exotique vous accueille.

from *Ce qu'il faut voir à l'Exposition coloniale*

Exhibit A: The Colonial Look

French press releases announcing that the 1931 Exposition coloniale internationale would leave its mark on haute couture spawned a flurry of articles in the fashion pages of American newspapers, suggesting that the event had managed to achieve the international status it sought. The *Detroit News* reported that "hats made using wood, coconut fiber, metal and paper" were making a splash and that "Arabian burnous" were popping up in the most fashionable European resorts as "a lounging robe for beach wear" (Feb. 4, 1931). Also direct from the Bois de Vincennes was jewelry "of the bright, barbaric type" (*New York City World*, Feb. 15, 1931) and a proliferation of bold "Algerian colors"—which, according to the fashion section of the *Seattle Times* (Feb. 23, 1931), included "red, yellow, blue, green, brown, orange, black and white": all colors were colonial, all ensembles exotic in the months leading up to the Exposition coloniale.

On the eve of decolonization, appropriations of the "colonial" in French cultural life reflected France's changing geopolitical role, as im-

Figure 2. *Trying colonialism on for size at the 1931 Exposition coloniale. Sygma/Keystone.*

perial rule gave way to postcolonial economic interdependency. On the face of it, there could not be a more conscious manifestation of colonial rhetoric than the Exposition coloniale, whose main function was to exhibit France's colonial empire to the rest of the world and, most important, to the French themselves. This exhibition, and others like it, constructed and promoted a unified identity for *la plus grande France*, imparting to the French a sense of belonging to a greater global community with a common purpose. Yet within this apparently homogeneous identity, a deep distinction was forged—in fact, the colonial empire's appearance of homogeneity was rooted in this distinction. Throughout the 1930s, representations of the colonial empire emphasized both difference (the exotic) and its domestication, paving the way for the postwar emergence of the "third world."

The most enduringly popular features of the colonial exhibitions were their human exhibits. People were routinely transported from the colonies for the purpose of "animating" the exhibitions, which usually involved performing an artisanal activity in a roped-off area before the

Figure 3. *An artisan on display in the colonial section of the 1937 World's Fair. Sygma/ Keystone.*

viewing public. Known as *cités indigènes* (native villages), these displays were designed to convey the look and feel of a native village. More significant, while introducing a largely Western audience to the workers—and consumers—who would play an increasingly important role in a changing global economy, these exhibits emphasized the distinction between colonizer and colonized, first world and third. The colonial exhibitions of the 1930s offered visitors living proof of the *mise en valeur* of the colonies—of the uses, in other words, to which a colonial empire could be put.[1]

WORKER CITIES

Walter Benjamin has noted that the world's fairs were the natural successors to the national industrial exhibitions (Benjamin 1978, 151–52). The exhibitions have always been a showcase for products. The worker cities, however, also made them showcases for the producers. Twentieth-century visitors to the colonial exhibitions could witness in the *cités indigènes* a microcosm of the new immigrant ghettoes developing in France, as the colonial map was gradually being superimposed onto the streets of French cities, which amassed their "taches roses" in the poorer sections of town. What visitors to the fairs could not see was the way exhibition organizers literally capitalized on the colonial displays.

The colonized people who were brought to the ECI and the 1937 World's Fair were confined to the fairgrounds for the duration of each exhibition. They lived and worked in the display pavilions and were not allowed to leave these areas without special permission from exhibition authorities.[2] The "Règlement intérieur du 6 mai 1931, article 3," specifies that these people

> answer to the superintendent of their division for matters of internal discipline. They are holders of identity cards provided to them by this commissioner. They are to be kept within the boundaries of their division at the time stated by their commissioner, in no case later than midnight. They may not leave the general Exhibition grounds unless they have a special pass granted to them by their supervisor, designated by the superintendent of the division. (Olivier 1933, 63)

In 1937, the colonized personnel were confined to the Ile des Cygnes, a narrow strip of land in the middle of the Seine, for the duration of the exhibition, which lasted six months, despite concerns voiced by one colonial official about "the unhygienic conditions of the banks of the Seine for the indigenous artisans accustomed to warmer countries, who will have to live there for several months" (Archives Nationales [A.N.] F12 12384, packet 1).

The "native villages" seem to have provided above all the means of controlling their residents. In a letter from Pierre Guesde, commissaire du Gouvernement Général de l'Indochine à l'Exposition, to the ministre des colonies, dated July 24, 1931, the writer refers to the *cité indigène* in the Indochinese section of the ECI: "Grouped as they are now, in a relatively restricted space surrounded by a barrier, the surveillance and control of their activities is obviously much easier and more efficient than if they had been scattered all over the place. Then they would have escaped from us entirely and become an easy target for the propagandists" (A.N. Aix, slotfom III / 5). In 1931, just a year after the Yen Bay uprising, the activities of the Indochinese contingent were of particular concern and were the object of especially close scrutiny by undercover security agents.[3] The police recruited Indochinese informants for the purpose of thwarting attempts to spread the doctrines of Ho Chi Minh. (This under-cover activity was denounced by the "Comité de Lutte des Indochinois contre l'Exposition Coloniale et les massacres en Indochine," which was also involved in the protest surrounding the plans to use rickshaws, pulled by Indochinese people brought over for the purpose, as a means of transporting visitors around the exhibition. The Ligue des Droits de l'Homme intervened, and exhibition organizers finally yielded to the protests.)

Like factory workers stationed in front of a moving assembly line, the colonized artisans remained fixed before the stream of visitors filing past them. Subjects of each colonial possession were required to remain in the area representing their country of origin. Perhaps not so coincidentally, this emphasis on order in the workplace recalls the famous dictum of Henri Fayol, whose *Administration industrielle et générale* was largely re-sponsible for popularizing the principles of Taylorism in France after the First World War: "Everyone knows the saying about keeping objects in order: *A place for everything and everything in its place.* The saying for so-cial order is identical: *A place for everyone and everyone in his place*" (Fayol 1979, 40; original emphasis). As well as evoking the confinement of the displaced personnel to the exhibition grounds, this statement can be read as a broader confirmation of social—and ethnic—hierarchies.

In one sense, the special pass required at the 1931 exhibition was an extension of the *carte de séjour*, which had been instituted as a require-ment for international residents of France in 1917. But the pass also bears a curious resemblance to the *livret* used by nineteenth-century employ-ers to keep tabs on their employees (see Gaudemar 1979, 114). Like many nineteenth-century workers, the colonized personnel lived in a kind of factory city, sleeping, eating, and working in the same enclosed space, which was wholly identified with the goods produced there.[4] A souvenir picture-book called *Merveilles de l'Exposition de 1937* announces that, in the Indochinese pavilion, "an effort has been made to arrange the arti-sans as they are back home. This is why we have Cotton Street, Cup Street, and Silk Lane" (Lange 1937, 40).

As it indicated in its official title, "L'Exposition internationale des arts et techniques dans la vie moderne," the 1937 World's Fair sought to val-orize a precapitalist or acapitalist mode of production. In the words of an official report generated by the organizers of the colonial section: "As in-dependent of capital as it is foreign to the notion of a salary, artisanry represents a form of work that is fully in keeping with our recognition of the liberty and dignity of the native" (*Rapport général de l'Afrique Equatoriale Française de l'Exposition internationale des arts et techniques, Paris 1937,* A.N. F12 12387, packet 1, p. 34). Yet in the same report we are told that the colonized artisans will in fact be wage laborers for the duration of the exhibition. The artisans from French Equatorial Africa, for example, received two hundred francs a month, which, when combined with the average commission earned by each artisan, amounted to one-fifth the monthly salary of the French cashier who worked in the shop that sold their products. They were closely monitored to make sure they did not sell any of their products themselves. Catherine Hodeir has pointed out that the colonial exhibitions provided, among other things, a metropolitan test market for goods produced in the colonies (Hodeir 1987, 289). Just as they were transplanted physically onto the Ile des Cygnes (or, in the case of the 1931 exhibition, to the Bois de Vincennes), the colonized producers were also transplanted into a capitalist economy—thus prefiguring the mass displacement of their children, less than a generation later, to the urban centers of France.

WHO'S LEFT?

The Exposition coloniale did not fail to elicit strong opposition from those who claimed to protect the rights of workers the world over. In 1931, members of the Parti Communiste français (PCF) distributed a pamphlet titled "Le véritable guide de l'Exposition coloniale: L'oeuvre civilisatrice de la France magnifiée en quelques pages" (The real guide to the Colonial Exhibition: France's civilizing mission clarified in a few pages). Several of the articles in this pamphlet are send-ups of procolonial propaganda. One announces: "35 années de bienfaits à Madagascar" (35 years of benefits to Madagascar)—and then lists examples of colonial repression in the country. Another article, "Les Sacrifices des grands sucriers à la Guadeloupe" (The sacrifices of the sugarcane plantation owners), begins:

> On February 12 of last year, the workers of the sugar plantations in Basse-Terre, who earned a colossal 7fr.50 (for the cane cutters), 5fr.70 (for dependent women), and 40 sous (for the kids), went on strike in demand of a pay raise! On February 25, the police responded, on the order of the plantation owners, to this intolerable pretension, by shooting at the doors and windows of workers' houses. . . . We should add that the profits of

the Colonial Sugar Company in 1925 attained only the measly sum of 26 million francs. (A.N. Aix-en-Provence, Slotfom III / 5 [s.d. 34]; unpaginated)

The PCF also distributed little slips of paper ("papillons") with anticolonial slogans printed on them at the exhibition. Slogans included "French imperialism constructs palaces in Vincennes. . . . But it has ravaged thousands of villages in Africa and Asia!"; "Colonialism is profitable for capitalists, but it has cost the lives of hundreds of thousands of French and native workers and peasants!"; and this dig at the socialists: "Colonial peoples are not asking for socialist-fascist governments. They are demanding independence" (A.N. Aix-en-Provence, Slotfom III / 5).

The Surrealists, too, articulated their opposition to colonialism using the language of Communism. The most notable collaboration between the two groups in opposition to the Exposition coloniale took the form of a counterexhibition. The Exposition anticoloniale, officially titled "La Vérité sur les colonies" (The truth about the colonies), was held in the fall of 1931 in the building that had been the "Pavillon des Soviets" at the 1925 Exposition des arts décoratifs de Paris (see Lebovics 1994). Sponsored by the Berlin-based Ligue anti-impérialiste and the French Secours Rouge and organized by the Surrealist André Thirion, the counterexhibition displayed charts and photographs denouncing, according to the guide, "colonialist hypocrisy" and "the fabulous profits made by exploiting the colonies." In one room, a display organized by Louis Aragon showed African, Oceanic, and Amerindian sculptures side by side with statues of the Christian Madonna and child, which were labeled "fétiches chrétiennes"—here, as ever, the Surrealists were aiming to decontextualize the familiar.

The Surrealists also published two tracts condemning the ECI. The first, dated May 1931 and titled "Ne Visitez pas l'Exposition coloniale" (Do not visit the Colonial Exhibition), was signed by Crevel as well as by Breton, Eluard, Benjamin Péret, Aragon, Yves Tanguy, and others. The pamphlet criticizes the hypocrisy of the exhibition and proposes a Communist alliance with colonial subjects the world over: "All those who refuse to be the eternal defenders of bourgeois nation-states will want to reject the trend toward pomp and exploitation in favor of the stance adopted by Lenin, who, at the beginning of this century, was the first to recognize colonized peoples as the allies of the global proletariat" (*Tracts surréalistes* 1980, 195). The second tract, "Premier bilan de l'Exposition coloniale" (first toll of the Colonial Exhibition), was written after a fire gutted the ECI's Dutch Indies pavilion, destroying priceless indigenous artworks. The tract asserts that the fire was the symbolic consummation of the imperialist destruction of indigenous culture: "So concludes the colonial project inaugurated by massacres and continued by means of religious proselytizing, forced labor, and illness" (Nadeau 1964, 331). To judge by the sarcastic tone of these tracts, the Surrealists had no trouble adopting the language of Communism.

Rather than argue, however, that the Surrealists adopted the Communist position on colonialism, it would be more accurate to say that the Surrealists aligned themselves with the Communist position at a particular moment of its development, because the PCF's line on colonialism was inconsistent. For all its sloganeering in 1931, the PCF's vocal resistance to imperialism was to erode by the second half of the decade. The vicissitudes of its position can be charted by comparing PCF-backed news coverage of the 1931 exhibition with coverage of the colonial section of the 1937 World's Fair.

In 1931, the Exposition coloniale served as the pretext for regular attacks on colonialism in the French Communist daily newspaper, L'Humanité, which marked a change from 1922, when the same paper's strategy had been to avoid all mention of the colonial exhibition in Marseille, doubtless to avoid publicizing it; instead, it increased its coverage of colonial atrocities appreciably in the weeks surrounding the exhibition's opening and referred to President Millerand as "le petit Alexandre" on more than one occasion when reporting on his trip to North Africa. In 1931, L'Humanité made a point of discussing the working conditions of the colonial participants at the colonial exhibition, "victims of a vile exploitation" who, having signed "a contract that binds them until October" (April 20), were prisoners of the "imperialist fair at Vincennes" (April 18, 19). Nearly all 1931 accounts in L'Humanité of colonial atrocities make some reference to the Exposition coloniale; and conversely, few articles covering the ECI fail to mention instances of imperialist brutality, as the following example attests: "At the foot of the temple of Angkor, Cambodian and Annamite standard-bearers in sumptuous costumes salute the chief of the colonial bandits who has just massacred their brothers yet again" (May 7, 1931).

In 1937, however, a remarkable change took place: L'Humanité promoted the Popular Front government's world's fair, for better or worse—including the colonial section. Depictions of the artisans, dancers, and other workers brought from colonized countries especially for the exhibition are more reminiscent of those found in the mainstream press than in a paper that, six years earlier, had decried their "vile exploitation." In an article of May 27, 1937, these people are described as if they were just another part of the scenery: "White pavilions on stilts succeed one another, with minarets and domes, pointed roofs, totemic figures, and striped facades [façades zébrées]. In the Moroccan pavilion, in a loggia, costumed natives play their instruments. Figures appear [apparaissent] in the diagonal slats of windows and behind veiled enclosures." The word "apparaissent" removes these people from their historical context, suggesting that they appear out of nowhere, peeking out from veiled partitions as if from behind a stage curtain. Similarly, adjectives such as "totémiques" and "zébrées" evoke an exoticized atmosphere, far removed from the viewing public.

Missing from L'Humanité in the weeks surrounding the inauguration of the 1937 exhibition are articles decrying colonial abuses, articles that were so prevalent in 1931, when exhibition propaganda and oppression were seen to go hand in hand. Given the preponderance and vehemence of such articles six years earlier, this lacuna is particularly conspicuous. It would not be difficult to attribute this phenomenon to the expression of professional loyalties: Blum, whose Popular Front government organized the 1937 World's Fair, had helped found L'Humanité, raising money on its behalf and contributing articles for a column titled "La Vie littéraire," before the paper became the mouthpiece of the French Communist Party in 1920. But the paper's change of perspective is more accurately seen as part of the left's response to the German threat. During Hitler's ascension to power, the colonial question, like most questions, became subsumed in the fascist question, and the PCF's position on colonization reflected this change of priorities.

As L'Humanité's inconsistent coverage of the three exhibitions attests, the PCF shifted its stance dramatically with regard to colonialism as the Second World War approached. The right-wing riot in Paris on February 6, 1934 marked a turning point in PCF policy; realizing that the imperative for a unified front against fascism outweighed the concessions they would have to make in collaborating with other parties, the French Communists signed a "pact of unified action" with the Socialist Party (which, while quick to denounce the use of military repression in the colonies, had never been opposed to the idea of colonial empire-building per se) on July 27, 1934. The resistance against capitalism was thus temporarily preempted by the struggle against fascism: in collaborating with various "bourgeois" parties to form the Popular Front, the PCF was breaking with its tradition of working-class leadership.

The temporary shift in emphasis away from class struggle can accordingly be observed in *L'Humanité*'s inconsistent treatment of the ties between capitalism and colonialism during the 1931 and 1937 exhibitions. In 1931, the paper did not fail to emphasize these ties, as in this article of May 7: "The Brun Biscuits and Citroen buildings show their facades as if to say that, at a capitalist fair, commercial promotion does not have to make any concessions. In addition, we can find the 'Moorish' pavilions of Félix Potin and the house of Picon" (2). No such potshots are taken in 1937; in fact, the word "capitalism" rarely appears, this notable omission reflecting the PCF's (fragile and short-lived) alliance with its former rival. Confronted by the fascist threat, the PCF not only put its revolutionary ideals on hold in order to combat fascism but also reversed its traditional policy of support for national independence movements in the colonies, on the grounds that, once independent, they would be fair game for Hitler and Mussolini (see Moneta 1971, 105 and passim).

By 1937, then, the French left no longer emphasized international worker solidarity, privileging instead its own national agenda. This focus on national concerns served to reinforce (and was reinforced by) the 1937 exhibition's implicit emphasis on the distinction between colonized workers and their French counterparts, an emphasis that becomes apparent when we compare the displays of the two groups at the 1937 World's Fair.

JOB PERFORMANCES

At the colonial section of the 1937 World's Fair, spectators were invited to behold the colonized participants in language that emphasized the voyeuristic aspect of the displays. The French public was not unaccustomed to the sight of human exhibits: in 1877, the Jardin d'Acclimation (zoological park) in Paris had added people, brought in from "exotic" locales across the globe, to its displays of animals and plants.[5] The world and colonial exhibitions, however, differed from the Jardin d'Acclimation displays in that they claimed to recreate the physical environments of the people exhibited, seeking to efface as much as possible the exhibition framework in order to encourage the suspension of disbelief. Whereas what attracted visitors to the Jardin d'Acclimation was the fact that the people on display had come from far away, visitors to the colonial and world exhibitions were supposed to feel as if they themselves had traveled to the ends of the earth. A book published for the occasion of the 1937 exhibition, *Voyages autour du monde*, begins, "In 1937, I circled the globe more than a hundred times at the world's fair" (Dupays 1938, 6).

The exhibition placed a special emphasis on the human displays in its colonial section:

> These swarming races that we have observed in their private lives [*dans leur vie intime*], in their daily existence [*dans leur existence quotidienne*], have shown us the magnitude of our "Empire" better than any speech or chart. They have made us see the enormous possibilities of our colonies, but they have also shown us the responsibilities that we must shoulder if we wish to preserve peace among these peoples and guarantee them the tranquil existence that we have been privileged to appreciate here in all its living realism [*dans tout son vivant réalisme*]. (Lange 1937, 40)

This desire to capture the "vie intime," the "existence quotidienne" of the colonized participants, the invocation of a "vivant réalisme," bespeak a turn away from self-consciously exhibitionist displays to a slice-of-life representational mode. The goal of such representations is to make viewers think that the people they are watching do not know they are being watched. An account of the African artisans provides a perfect example of this representational mode:

> The good-natured curiosity of visitors encourages the artists from the Gabon, the Middle Congo, Oubangui, and Chad who work before the eyes [*sous les yeux*] of the public: they admire the good ivory worker who fashions a pipe, another who polishes a bracelet; then there is a cobbler seated on a mat, vigorously polishing the yellow boots he has just finished making, beautiful boots that will doubtless become the property of a hunter; across from him, a tailor sews quietly, without seeming to notice us [*sans avoir l'air de s'apercevoir de notre présence*]. (Thomarel 1937, unpaginated)

The artisans cannot be unaware of the crowds of people who watch them work; yet the phrase "sans avoir l'air de s'apercevoir de notre présence" turns what would otherwise be an exhibition in the literal sense into the object of a voyeuristic fantasy. In being depicted as the unwitting objects of the public's gaze, the artisans are deprived of the possibility of looking back, of becoming the subjects of their own gaze. They are locked into an unreciprocal relationship that objectifies them, establishing an unbreachable barrier between observer and observed. The expression "sous les yeux" serves as a constant reminder of the imaginary but infinite distance separating the human exhibits from their viewers. Ironically, then, the voyeuristic fantasy, which is grounded in the illusion of intimacy, serves to reinforce the division between observer and observed, colonizer and colonized.

The specular dimension of colonialism is characteristic of what Tony Bennett has called the exhibitionary complex, or the emergence, throughout the nineteenth century, of institutions such as museums, department stores, arcades, and international exhibitions, which functioned as vehicles for the circulation of developing disciplines such as history, biology, art history, and anthropology and for the regulation of social order. In contrast to Foucault's model of the "carceral archipelago" (Foucault 1979, 298), in which regulatory functions were withdrawn from public inspection to the confines of prisons and other "correctional" sites, Bennett's model emphasizes the extent to which the display of power became an increasingly public event. Bennett places particular emphasis on the imperial function of the exhibitionary complex, in which the display of peoples deemed primitive in anthropological museums and world's fairs served to "underlin[e] the rhetoric of progress by serving as its counterpoint" (Bennett 1988, 92). The institutions comprising the exhibitionary complex deployed a "technology of vision which served not to atomize and disperse the crowd but to regulate it, and to do so by rendering it visible to itself, by making the crowd itself the ultimate spectacle" (81).

Between the complex's imperial function and its role as a mirror of the masses, however, there is a cleavage that Bennett does not account for. Although he points out that the observation of subjected peoples reinforced ethnic hierarchies and cultural domination, his analysis takes into account only the (French) crowd's relation to itself, without considering the relation between the crowd and the objects of its gaze. Collective "self"-observation and the observation of people coded as different, as "other," may be mutually reinforcing—indeed, interdependent—acts, but they are not equatable. For, whereas in the case of self-observation it is quite accurate to say that "the exhibitionary complex . . . perfected a self-monitoring system of looks in which the subject and object positions can be exchanged," no possibility of symbolic reciprocity exists when the object of the gaze is not (the same as) the subject, when, instead, it is subjected to the gaze (Bennett 1988, 82). (I say no possibility of *symbolic* reciprocity because, although there is nothing preventing the objects of such a gaze from looking back, their spectatorship would nonetheless not result in their "seeing themselves from the side of power" [76].) Rather than pose as an alternative to the "carceral" model, the displays of colonized people at the colonial exhibitions exemplified it. Bennett writes that "the exhibitionary complex was also a response to the problem of order, but one which worked differently [from Foucault's carceral model] in seeking to transform that problem into one of culture—a question of winning hearts and minds as well as the disciplining and training of bodies" (76). It must be asked, To whom do these respective hearts, minds, and bodies belong? In the colonial context, the "problem of order" was transferred to the people on display: the hearts and minds being won over may have been French, but the bodies being disciplined were those of the colonized (as their rigid confinement and control, described above, suggest).

The modes of spectatorship engendered by this power differential become clear when descriptions of colonial artisans are compared with descriptions of French people performing similar functions. This opportunity for comparison is provided by the Regional and Rural Centers of the 1937 World's Fair, where visitors could watch French artisans performing many tasks similar to those of their colonial counterparts. Just as on the Ile des Cygnes, artisanal work was valorized at the Rural and Regional Centers; but whereas the colonized artisans were represented in voyeuristic descriptions as *objects* that were valuable to the extent that they could be put to use, French artisans were represented as *subjects* for French visitors to identify with in a time of crisis. The effects of the 1929 stock market crash had reached France later than most other industrialized countries, but they also took longer to dissipate: at a time when other industrialized countries were beginning to regain economic stability, France had still not recovered from the depression. Throughout the 1930s, industrial unemployment slowed urban growth, forcing a significant number of people back to rural communities, where they lived off the land or engaged in other subsistence activities (Berstein 1988, 7–8). These activities were represented by the blacksmiths, weavers, and potters at the Centre régional and the Centre rural.

Forms of the expression "sous vos yeux," which appear so often in accounts of the colonized artisans, can also occasionally be found in descriptions of French artisanal displays. In a speech made at the inauguration of the Picardy Pavillon on July 23, 1937, general organizer Gaston Midy depicts Picardy's artisanal exhibit in much the same way that the artisanal exhibits of the colonies are described: "The artisanal division will feature, before our very eyes [*sous nos yeux*], two working artisanal centers with which you are already familiar [*que vous connaissez bien*]" (*Rapport général* for the AEF section of the 1937 exhibition, A.N. F12 12387, p. 138). Yet in this case, the alienation suggested by the expression "sous nos yeux" is tempered by the restrictive clause "que vous connaissez bien," which evokes a familiarity absent in depictions of the colonized artisans. Midy's speech continues: "In these two centers, as yet untouched by automation, the artisan is at home, in surroundings whose general structure has not changed for centuries. The reconstruction [*reconstitution*] on display represents the actual work site of a weaver from Bohain, a worker whose life is carefree, filled with work and healthy pleasures" (138). Although the insistence on the weaver's happy-go-lucky lifestyle is no doubt unrealistic, nowhere is it implied that the artisan is unaware of the public's presence. The impression is conveyed rather that he is inviting the public to share in his joy: the workplace is the scene of a "reconstitution," a "représent[ation]," in which the artisan is an exhibitionist, a willing participant in a "job performance" rather than the unwitting object of a voyeuristic gaze. The French artisan's demonstration is perceived as educational, edifying—but similar demonstrations performed by colonized artisans are denied a pedagogical function:

> Indeed, the visiting masses get less out of a lesson, however lively it may be, than an attraction, especially one that involves individuals of the black race.
>
> And that is why the artisans of Equatorial Africa, working before the eyes of the public, have had so much success. (*Rapport général* for the AEF section of the 1937 exhibition, A.N. F12 12387, pp. 63–64)

The possibility that the colonial artisans could teach spectators a "leçon des choses" was rejected in favor of attributing to them carnivalistic status as an "attraction." Pedagogical roles were reserved for French artisans; the colonial participants were relegated to the sideshow.

The differences between representations of the French artisans and those of their colonial counterparts on the Ile des Cygnes are apparent even in the most seemingly peripheral details: in an article describing the native village in the French West African section of the ECI, the author notes that "in these houses work the best native artisans, who continue [*continuer*] to fashion, before the eyes of visitors, the traditional brightly colored loincloths" (Angoulvant 1931, 838). The verb "continuer" suggests that the artisans are doing what they would have been doing had there been no one to watch them, and that they are carrying on *in spite of* the presence of spectators who have wandered in to observe them. In the same article, even a dance performance becomes the object of a voyeuristic fantasy when it is executed by "des groupes de danseurs et de danseuses, venues [*sic*] de la Côte d'Ivoire et de la Haute-Guinée, [qui] se livrent sous vos yeux à des ébats chorégraphiques" (groups of dancers who have come from the Ivory Coast and New Guinea to engage in choreographed frolics before your very eyes) (Angoulvant 1931, 838). Here the dancers are not dancing; they are engaging in graceful paroxysms (*ébats*). Spectators are no longer an audience attending a performance but rather peeping toms being let in on a private, playful moment (the feminine participle "venues," grammatically awkward in its context, turns the whole scene into a heterosexual male fantasy).

A similar distinction between French and colonial artisans is made in the exhibition's *Guide officiel*. Spectators who did not tire of watching others work could also visit the exposition's Centre rural, described in the following terms:

> You are now entering the City of Trades and Artisanry, which includes twenty-two artisanal houses, each comprising a different trade, grouped around a sumptuous palace. These dwellings—the glassblower's house, above which rise three large glass balls that reflect the play of light, and the engraver's house, the cabinet maker's, the ceramist's, the potter's, the printer's, the blacksmith's—have been constructed with a demonstrative purpose in mind [*dans un but démonstratif*]. You will see the artisan "labor" ["*oeuvrer*"] in the milieu he knows best and which corresponds to his needs for work and comfort. (*Exposition internationale des arts et techniques: Guide officiel* 1937, 147)

Although the rural artisans are here the object of the public's gaze, the quotation marks placed around the word "oeuvrer" suggest that it is not work that's being watched but rather a representation of work—"dans un but démonstratif." The real work required of the French artisans is not their labor so much as the representation, or staging, of that labor. For the duration of their participation in the exhibition, they are actors, even though they are "performing" the same functions they will continue to carry out when the exhibition has ended.

The section that the *Guide officiel* devotes to the Centre régional tends to emphasize the regional products much more than their producers; however, visitors to the Pavillon de la Vallée Moyenne de la Loire were informed that "in the Trades room, you will observe the [*vous assisterez au*] work of a Levalois weaver on an old loom, a Choletais potter, a Saumorois medal maker" (106). The verb "assister à" clearly emphasizes the performative aspect of the weaver's display. The expression "before your eyes" is reserved, in the *Guide officiel*, for the colonized artisans ("The Cambodians execute, before your eyes, the marvelous objects in finely worked silver" [100]); in fact, in the section on the Regional Center, the verb "voir" is used exclusively with reference to inanimate objects or representations of animals: for example, "There you will see [*vous y voyez*], beneath the staircase, a diorama of the Loire with golden sands, as well as photographs and models of prizewinning animals" (106). Spectators "attend" a live performance by an actor who is aware of their presence, but they "see" representations that cannot return their gaze. Looking assumes an objectifying function, reserved for things and animals that can be domesticated, dominated—as the preposition "sous" in the expression "sous vos yeux" suggests. This association is retained when the verb "voir" is applied to the inhabitants of the Ile des Cygnes, as in the description of feeding time: "Restaurants serve the natives their customary food, and it will be possible for you to see them eat [*il vous sera loisible de les voir manger*] pungent dishes out of little bowls and tiny cups, as if in the presence of the traveling soup merchants of the Far East" (100). The animal analogy is made explicit in a 1931 issue of *Le Monde colonial illustré*: "Of all the exotic animals that you can observe at the Colonial Exhibition, it is still man who is the most interesting" (cited in Palà 1981, 24).

Statements such as these reveal how colonial discourse "looks"—in both the active and passive senses of the word. They illustrate the reifying effect of the voyeuristic gaze that was invited (and presupposed) at the colonial exhibitions of the 1930s. These cultural events prepared spectators for the increasingly important role of the third world in a changing global economy, a world whose labor (in the postwar period) and whose export markets (after decolonization) would be appropriated as readily as the "bright, barbaric" jewelry that changed the face of fashion for a brief moment between the wars.

Exhibit B: Miss France d'Outre-Mer, 1937

The voyeuristic gaze elicited at the colonial exhibitions was not limited to descriptions of artisans at work. It also assumed a more overtly sexualized function, as witnessed by accounts of a beauty contest held on the Ile des Cygnes in 1937. One coffee-table book of the period explains:

> The ten beauties competing for the coveted title of Miss Overseas France [*Miss France d'Outre-Mer*], all elected in their countries of origin, are each the product of a union between a French man and a woman from the colonies, or, what's much less common, between a French woman and a male native. These are hybrids [*métisses*], with the exception of one of them, a splendid Creole of the white race from Réunion Island who, for this reason, knows that she is out of the running. (Dupays 1938, 271)

Miss Réunion Island, by virtue of her white skin, has an unfair advantage over the other, less fortunate contestants; she is disqualified in the interest of fairness but put on display so that spectators can behold her "admirable" beauty. Ironically, she stands out from her peers precisely because she is not different enough—too much "France," not enough "overseas." Yet the winner of the contest cannot be *too* different, as the same account suggests: "The panel of judges bestows the title of Miss Overseas France upon the Guadeloupean, Miss Casalan, whose skin is as pale as ivory" (272). The winner must be as white as possible, without being so white that she would be "out of the running." She must be white enough to conform to French standards of beauty, yet she must retain the mark of difference that makes her exotic.

What this event ultimately exhibits, besides flesh, is the tension between identity and difference that characterized French imperial rhetoric throughout the Third Republic. It is the literal embodiment, or representation through the body, of the assimilation debate that not only informed France's colonial relations but also played a defining role in its relations with other world powers. The identity that France was perpetually constructing in connection with those countries it dominated culturally, politically, and militarily reinforced the aggressive image it sought to convey to countries that posed a military threat to France, particularly Germany. This dual position, which might be deemed at once offensive and defensive, can be read in the beauty contest's title, in which the word "Miss," which reflects the foreign origins of this cultural event, undermines the hegemonic pretensions of the expression "France d'Outre-Mer."[6]

Colonialism and nationalism converged explicitly in the proposal for the Miss Overseas France contest ("Concours du Meilleur Mariage Colonial, Exposé du projet," dated April 15, 1936), which pitted France

Figure 4. *"Miss France d'Outre-Mer" contestants, L'Ile des Cygnes, 1937.* L'Illustra-tion's *caption reads: "Miss France d'Outre-mer and her competitors, young métisse beau-ties from the French Empire. . . . Five young women of Franco-Asiatic blood (Misses Tonkin, Annam, Cochinchina, Laos, and Pondicherry) against five young women of Franco-African blood (Misses Madagascar, Senegal, Guadeloupe, Martinique, and Guyana), flanked by the daughter of the senator of Réunion Island, Miss Réunion, who did not compete, lone white rose on this colorful rosebush. Miss Guadeloupe, a magnificent brown rose, was elected nearly unanimously . . . , but Miss Annam and Miss Tonkin, rav-ishing yellow roses, also had their admirers."* L'Illustration, *Sygma/Keystone.*

against Germany in a battle of birthrates: "We are suffering from a terri-fying deficiency [*hémorragie*] in birthrate (700,000 babies a year vs. 1,200,000 in Germany), and all the remedies attempted in order to stop this hemorrhage have failed. Perhaps our colonial empire of 60 million inhabitants offers us the final remedy, by the amalgamation of these pro-lific races with ours" (A.N. F12 12258). This was not the first time France had appealed to its colonial empire for a solution to its manpower prob-lem: the reliance on colonial subjects, particularly West Africans, as sol-diers in World War I has been well documented.[7] Rather than solicit bodies for the purpose of bolstering troop numbers, however, this pro-posal envisages another function for them—as reproductive partners.

The emphasis on comparative birthrates in the contest proposal re-flected a persistent French preoccupation with *dénatalité* (declining birthrate), the vestiges of which can be seen in France today in the discounts for "familles nombreuses" (large families) offered at movie theaters and zoos. This preoccupation resulted in the increasing rhetorical value placed on maternity through the first decades of the twentieth century (see Thébaud in Thalmann 1986). The contestants vying for the title of Miss France d'Outre-Mer represented motherhood doubly: first, by virtue of their status as products of "mariages coloniaux" (colonial marriages), and second—because beauty contests are designed to appeal to men—by virtue of their status as potential producers in a future union. The Miss France proposal reflects this double status, as well as the equation of beauty and racial compatibility that was to be the ultimate justification for the contest:

> But should we encourage this amalgamation, and if so, with which races? Should we discourage mixtures with certain races? Between the Spanish colonial doctrine, which practiced this interbreeding, and the English doctrine, which abhors it, France could create *Distinguos* according to race. A young French bureaucrat or businessman who settles in the colonies would know which races to marry with ours by their beauty, and which abort in ugliness [*celles qui avortent en laideur*]. ("Concours," A.N. F12 12258)

The use of the verb "avorter" here to describe unsuitable marriage partners is extremely suggestive, especially coming just a few sentences after France's declining birthrate was described as a "hémorragie," a term that stands out not only because of its illustrative force but also because it is used improperly: a hemorrhage is the loss of something that already exists, not the failure to create something that does not yet exist. This passage exemplifies what Alice Yaeger Kaplan has called the "abortion anxiety" that took hold of France between the wars (Kaplan 1986, 101–6). Abortion and contraception had been illegal in France since 1920, the year in which, not uncoincidentally, a governmental decree had established a series of medals to be awarded to mothers of large families (Bell and Offen 1983, 306–10).

Motherhood and the national obsession with race also converged at another display at the 1937 World's Fair, titled "La Famille, la Femme, l'Enfant," whose promotional claims were cited by a popular women's magazine: "Here we ask you to consider, compassionately and seriously, the most important problem of our era," to which was added this parenthetical comment: "The most important indeed, because it concerns the future of our race" (*Eve* 874, June 27, 1937, p. 3). A problem conceived in terms of the future of a "race," whose solution lay, as the organizer of the beauty contest claimed, in determining which were the right "amalgamations," made perfect sense at an exhibition that included a section devoted to the triple theme of sports, physical education, and eugenics (*Le livre d'or officiel* . . . 1938, 151). Here improvement of the individual was linked in no uncertain terms to the improvement of the race.

In official documents, the Miss France d'Outre-Mer contest was referred to as the "Concours du Meilleur Mariage Colonial" (Best colonial marriage contest) and pitched as "a demonstration of eugenics" ("Extrait certifié," in "Dossier relatif aux comptes du Comité du Meilleur Mariage Colonial," A.N. F12 12258, packet 3). The desire to determine which were the "best" marriages was a logical extension of *puériculture*, a term used by eugenicists to denote "questions of heredity and selection in their application to the human species." An outgrowth of the natalist organizations of the 1890s, which united conservatives concerned about the declining birthrate and Catholics opposed to birth control, the *puériculture* movement appealed to a wide variety of health professionals through its advocacy of measures ranging from prenatal care and breastfeeding to the institution of a requirement for premarital health examinations. Were it not for what William H. Schneider calls their "hereditarian underpinnings" (Schneider 1990a, 72), such proposals would amount to little more than sound medical advice. A preoccupation with "biological regeneration," however, blurred the boundaries between well-baby care and social engineering, resulting in the motto "puericulture before procreation," which expanded prenatal care to include considerations of the moral as well as the physical influence of ancestry. The physicians, statisticians, and public health officials who founded the French Eugenics Society in 1912 usually limited their recommendations for "social hygiene" to campaigns against alcoholism and disease, but there were also those who advocated restrictions on immigration and the sterilization of "undesirables" (Schneider 1990a, 75).

It would seem that the separatist exhortations of the eugenicists contradicted the inclusive discourse of the advocates of *métissage*. Actually, however, these ideas had a great deal in common—so much so, in fact, that they were propounded within yards of one another at the same cultural event: the 1937 World's Fair. Organized by the Institut International d'Anthropologie, the Premier Congrès Latin d'Eugénique (whose very title indicates a predilection for dividing the world into neat categories) met August 1–3, 1937, in conjunction with the Exposition internationale. Founded in 1935, the International Latin Federation of Eugenics Societies had been conceived as an alternative to the International Eugenics Federation, which in the thirties was dominated by the Nazis and the Americans (Schneider 1990a, 97). This "alternative," as it turns out, was not much of one. Proposals designed to increase the population coexisted with those intended to restrict it; the two perspectives converged in the concept of ethnic purity, whose popularity coincided with the sharp rise in immigration after World War I. The eugenicists, bolstered by the popular writings of racial theorists such as Alexis Carrel and Joseph-Arthur de Gobineau (whose *Essai sur l'inégalité des races humaines* attained its height of popularity only after the turn of the century, although it was first published in 1853), sought to reinforce the racial divisions they deemed natural by cloaking their theories of racial hierarchies in the positivistic language of the biological sciences.

One of the speakers at the conference held at the 1937 World's Fair was a Dr. Georges Schreiber, who held various leadership roles in the French Eugenics Society throughout his career. Schreiber presented a paper titled "Allocations familiales et eugénique [*sic*]" (Familial and eugenic incentives) in which he advocated a system of financial subsidies designed to promote what he considered to be desirable marriages: "We believe it possible to produce eugenic effects from the Familial Incentives. In order to affect the quality of the population, it would be best to raise the amounts of the incentives each time the parents, upon examination, were considered to be desirable procreators, and providing that the children they bring into the world were deemed healthy, vigorous, and unblemished by hereditary defect" (*Rapport du Premier Congrès* 1937, 99). Lest there be any confusion about the origins of these ideas, René Martial, who also spoke at the conference, took pains to distinguish French eugenics from that practiced by the Germans—but he was equally anxious to distance himself from what he called the "laisser-aller" (free-for-all) of unions based solely on mutual attraction:

The two most widely held opinions today concerning interbreeding are the following. Either we return to the old idea of some long-lost purity and consequently the formal exclusion of certain races—examples: the massacre of the redskins [*peaux-rouges*] by the Americans, the expulsion of the Marranos of Spain by Philip II and that of the Jews by Hitler—or, we settle for chaos and anarchy, we say the mixing of races is inoffensive and we fail to see why love cannot be the sole guide between a Chinese man and a French or American woman. Both theories, that of exclusivity as well as that of a free-for-all [*laisser-aller*], are equally bad; because, if there are good mixtures, there are also very bad ones. (25)

French eugenics was to provide a happy medium between the equally abhorrent excesses of genocide and reproductive freedom.

While the Miss France d'Outre-Mer contest was busy crowning one of the "good mixtures"—indeed, the "best"—scientists at the eugenics conference were warning against those deemed "very bad." Martial, a public health physician and lecturer at the Institut d'Hygiène de la Faculté de Médecine de Paris, was known for using the biochemical index of blood types devised by Ludwik and Hannah Hirszfeld to develop an influential theory of "interracial grafting." This index showed a higher proportion of type B blood among non-Europeans, which prompted Martial to recommend the following guidelines for immigration policy: "Keep the O's and the A's, eliminate the B's, and keep the AB's if the psychological and health examination is favorable" (Schneider 1990b, 248).[8] In the paper he presented at the world's fair, Martial invoked his expertise on the subject of blood type in order to provide examples illustrating the danger posed by certain combinations. These examples are worth citing at length:

> Case 1. A Creole man marries a French woman and they have three daughters. The eldest daughter herself has four healthy children; the second marries a Jew, and one of their two children, a boy, is severely retarded. This is a case of interbreeding [*métissage*] between already mixed blood and blood of Asiatic origin.
>
> Case 2. A Jew marries an English woman. Their daughter marries a Frenchman. This marriage produces three boys, all three healthy. Two of them remain single, and one marries and has five children: four solid, healthy boys and a backward daughter [*une fille idiote*]. A case of intermingling of Asiatic blood and Occidental blood.
>
> Case 3. A Frenchman marries an Asian woman [*une orientale* (*sic*)]. They have four children. The eldest is a known mythomaniac and almost dangerous. A case of mixing French and Asiatic blood.
>
> Case 4. A Frenchman marries an Asian woman with whom he has a son and two daughters. The eldest daughter appears normal—but marries a Chinese man. Was it the instinct of the B-type bloods that compelled her? (*Rapport du premier Congrès* 1937, 30)

Martial's point is clear: unsavory unions such as these produce grotesquely abnormal offspring, ranging from a man known to embellish the truth, to a woman who appears to be normal but marries a Chinese. Using this logic, Martial advocates the institution of a "sélection sévère" (rigorous selection) in immigration policy.

It is apparent from the examples he cites that one of the groups targeted for exclusion by Martial is the Jews. Despite his condemnation of Hitler for putting into practice such a policy, his own suggestion that the union of Jews and non-Jews can only produce disastrous results amounts to implying that segregating the Jews would be an important part of the effort to improve the French "race." The long history of specifically French antisemitism notwithstanding, Martial's insinuations situate him closer to Hitler than his efforts to carve out a place for a national eugenics movement would suggest. (This affinity would leave the realm of abstraction and innuendo some five years later, as the Vichy government rounded up thousands of French Jews to send them to concentration camps; see Marrus and Paxton 1981). Ironically, Martial is unable convincingly to differentiate himself from Hitler precisely to the extent that he insists on differentiating among ethnic groups.

In his persistent quest to uncover difference in disguise, Martial also studied the family trees of certain monarchs who displayed signs of mental illness, tracing their ancestry back, in some cases five hundred years, until he found evidence of a "mixed" marriage by which to account for the future abnormality (*Rapport du premier Congrès* 1937, 30). (His determination to locate difference at the root of all evil no doubt caused him to overlook the more obvious fact that, on the contrary, sickly royals are most often the product of a genetic *lack* of difference.) This arbitrary imposition of difference—like Martial's attempt to differentiate himself from Hitler even while advocating Hitlerian policies, and his exclusionary attribution of difference to certain ethnic groups—is the flipside of the equally contrived imposition of homogeneity implicit in the eugenicists' claims to French racial unity.

At first glance, the attempts by one branch of the scientific community to maintain barriers between ethnic groups may seem strangely at odds with the collapse of such barriers promoted at the Best Colonial Marriage contest. Yet the dichotomy between the separatism advocated by the physicians and anthropologists at the eugenics conference and the *métissage* promoted by the beauty contest is a false one. These positions in fact comprised complementary aspects of the same discourse—a discourse that informed the debate over two seemingly divergent but actually inseparable components of French colonial administrative policy: assimilation and association.

The tension between identity and difference in colonial discourse was made visible at the Miss France d'Outre-Mer contest, which promoted an ideal that consisted of equal parts exoticism and familiarity. In order to be intelligible, difference had to be brought home to the viewing audience; it had, in other words, to be domesticated.

The domestication of difference played a major role in scenarios that involved gender as well as those involving race. By billing contestants as the offspring of a *French man* and a *colonial woman*, the Miss France d'Outre-Mer pageant evoked the age-old allegory of the feminized colony offering herself up for the enjoyment of a masculine empire. The colonized partner in the "best" colonial marriage could only be female, just as the picture-perfect product of such a union could only be female, because the reverse scenario, in which French women were invited to desire colonial men, would pose too great a threat to the pattern of domination built into both gender roles and colonial relations.[9] In a context that entails the viewing of the less powerful by the more powerful, the act of looking can only confirm the inequality of the relationship—that is, it can only be objectifying.

It is for this reason that a classic text in feminist film theory, Laura Mulvey's "Visual Pleasure and Narrative Cinema," can be useful here, despite the obvious differences between a "live" visual experience and a film.[10] To the extent that Mulvey's essay can enhance our understanding of the imbalance of power cultivated by certain specular configurations that play on sexual difference, it can certainly provide a framework within which to consider a beauty contest designed to appeal to men. But the essay can also serve to illuminate the domestication of other differences—in this case, racial—at work in the same spectacle.

Mulvey's emphasis on narrative structure foregrounds the effects produced by certain visual expressions of temporality. The spectacle of colonial women on display would at first glance seem to exist outside linear time (in other words, as an image that is removed from a narrative context), creating what Mulvey describes as the fetishistic scopophilia that confers gratification in the mere sight of the object (1986, 205). But the contestants vying for recognition as the product of the Best Colonial Marriage do, in fact, come equipped with a past: each bears witness to a tropical romance between a (fearless) French male colonist and an (exotic) indigenous woman. The narrative thus implied, according to Mulvey, would turn the specular relationship into one of voyeurism, whose sadistic aspect she explains by referring to a familiar Freudian landmark, castration: "[For the voyeur], pleasure lies in ascertaining guilt (immediately associated with castration), asserting control and subjugating the guilty person through punishment or forgiveness" (205). Unable to accept the lack of resemblance to himself that he encounters on seeing a woman's genitals, the voyeur must explain this difference in terms of a deficient similarity, imagining that the woman he observes has voluntarily put an end to the originary resemblance he ascribes to her—imagining, in other words, that she has castrated herself. The male spectator who assigns blame for the creation of such phantasmatic lack is indeed himself the perpetrator of the crime; the guilt that he "ascertains" in the woman is his own, which he has projected onto her.

In the colonial context, the phantasmagorical conversion of difference into lack takes skin color as its object. Racial complexes function like phallocentrism to the extent that they read the presence of melanin as the absence of whiteness, just as the presence of female sexual organs is represented negatively as the lack of a male sexual organ. The positing of a French (or an Aryan) race as a normative unit in relation to which other races are degenerate is analogous to Freud's designation of the feminine as a deviation from the masculine norm. It is at the juncture of these racist and masculinist discourses that the Miss France d'Outre-Mer contest must be situated.

The relationship cultivated between observers and observed at the Best Colonial Marriage contest was not unlike that between France and its colonies: the closer they got to one another, the more apparent it became that there was an insurmountable barrier between them. The act of bringing them together did not create the barrier; it just made it visible. Because the colonies were yoked to France in a relationship of domination, there was no way they could be either fully assimilated or free to associate with France—neither fully included in French political life nor entirely autonomous from it. Likewise, what French men (and, to a certain extent, French women and colonial spectators of both sexes who had internalized the subjection they experienced) saw when they looked at "overseas French" women was determined by the set of political and sexual relations already in place.

The spectacle of the Best Colonial Marriage contest contained both an irreducibly nonmetaphorical significance—that of the position of women of color in the political and social structures of colonialism—and an allegorical one—that of the nationalist fear of emasculation by Germany which had been invoked in order to justify France's emasculation of its colonial possessions. By definition, imperialist assertions of superiority entail the conversion of difference into lack. Like the voyeurism elicited by one of the most celebrated national icons, Marianne in her ill-fitting bodice, the Miss France d'Outre-Mer contest repeated in microcosm the projection of guilt onto the object(s) whose subjection was desired.

In 1936, the prominent geneticist Lucien Cuénot, who was among those urging the French government to upscale its efforts to redress the declining birthrate, warned prophetically: "France, headed towards ruin by its absence of a family policy, would make a very nice German colony" (quoted in Schneider 1990a, 97). His prophecy was to be borne out sooner than he might have thought possible, as the merits of assimilation and association were debated at the border between occupied France and Vichy.

❧

CHAPTER 2

Raymond Roussel and the Structure of Stereotype

When you see how the people live, and still more, how easily they die, it is always difficult to believe that you are walking among human beings. All colonial empires are in reality founded upon that fact. The people have brown faces—besides, they have so many of them! Are they really the same flesh as yourself? Do they even have names? Or are they merely a kind of undifferentiated brown stuff, about as individual as bees or coral insects?

George Orwell, "Marrakech"

As the colonial exhibitions demonstrated, the ideological conversion of difference into lack made possible the collaboration between expansion and exclusion that characterized French colonialism at its "apogee." The colonial exhibitions made a spectacle of this collaboration, promoting cultural contact in order, paradoxically, to reinforce the divisions among groups. A similar tension between identity and difference was played out less overtly, but at least as forcefully, in the work of Raymond Roussel, the eccentric author who was a source of inspiration to avant-garde movements such as Surrealism and Oulipo but who was not himself attached to any particular group.

Roussel forged his own path literally as well as figuratively, traveling all over Europe in a custom-built mobile home (a precursor of the modern-day Winnebago) fitted with a fringed velvet armchair and a kitchen. But here, as in his literary works, his interest in other cultures was oddly superficial: in his celebrated novel *Impressions d'Afrique*, Africa provides no more than a backdrop for exploits that could take place anywhere (or, more accurately, nowhere at all, so outlandish were they); and, although his travels took him far and wide, Roussel boasted about the fact that he never left his mobile home. This led family friend Michel Leiris to conclude that "Roussel never really traveled in any meaningful sense of the word" (1964, 77–78). Roussel insisted that he took no literary inspiration from his travels, creating his bizarre assortment of characters and plots ex nihilo (Roussel 1995, 27). His "impressions" of Africa and of other colonial spots were a product of his imagination: following from afar Leiris's Mission Dakar-Djibouti, which he had helped finance, Roussel was, in many ways, a velvet-fringed armchair anthropologist.

Roussel's mobile home is a fitting allegory of his literary project, which involved traveling everywhere and arriving nowhere. His work, in all its disparate forms (poetry, novels, theater), is unified by a preponderance of narrative layers and labyrinthine digressions. In the first Surrealist Manifesto, Breton writes that Roussel "is Surrealist as a storyteller" (Breton 1972, 27) (the French gives "Roussel est surréaliste dans l'anecdote"). All of Roussel's longer works overflow with stories and anecdotes so numerous as to be impossible to keep straight. The presence of this trait in his theater caused particular frustration because the plays did not conform to a dramatic convention that privileged showing over telling.

Roussel turned to the theater after failing to gain the recognition he sought from his novels and poetry. This shift began when he adapted his novels *Impressions d'Afrique* and *Locus Solus* for the stage, hoping to appeal to a wider audience. These productions did not meet with much success, however; and the plays he subsequently mounted that had been written expressly for the stage, *L'Étoile au front* (The star on the forehead) and *Poussière de soleils* (Sun dust), were even less successful—or, rather, theirs was a succès de scandale—causing the kind of uproar that had previously greeted Jarry's *Ubu roi* and Hugo's *Hernani*.[1] Audiences found Roussel's theater unsuited to the stage; and indeed, there is little about the plays that is specifically theatrical. The pieces are actually a series of stories told in dialogue form, narratives that are, moreover, what Gérard Genette calls "hétérodiégétiques," or unrelated to the characters recounting them (1969, 202). Rather than represent events, Roussel's plays represent the *representation* of events; they show the telling of stories. As such, they are the very enactment of the colonial unconscious: while the attention is focused in one place, the story unfolds elsewhere.[2]

Roussel privileged the latent over the patent both in his literary works and in the method he used to write many of them. The twinned themes of secrecy and discovery run through both *L'Étoile au front* and *Poussière de soleils*: in the former, several anecdotes indicate the discovery of traits that point to previously undisclosed ethnic differences, and in the latter, a treasure hunt leads not only to the discovery of a treasure but also to the discovery of a hidden past that allows the discoverers to carve out an identity for themselves. But most spectacularly, the theme of secrecy casts a dazzling shadow over Roussel's literary practice. First, the publication, immediately after his death, of *Comment j'ai écrit certains de mes livres* revealed the key to Roussel's method of creation (a secret whose existence was not even known until its unmasking); and then, in the late 1980s, the discovery of several trunks—a treasure trove—full of unpublished and previously unknown manuscripts added to the aura of mystery surrounding the author.

Included among these unpublished works was a never-performed play, *La Seine*, thought to have been written between 1900 and 1903. Although the play lies outside the chronological scope of this book, it is worth noting the presence of a scene that prefigures Roussel's theater of the interwar period, perfectly encapsulating the tension between national and racial identity. In this exchange, "Armand, nègre"—the only character out of hundreds in the play to have an epithet attached to his name—provokes a crisis of classification:

IRMA ACARY
No!!! You're not French!
ARMAND, NEGRO
Yes I am.
IRMA
You're not a real negro.
ARMAND
Of course I am.
IRMA
And in your country people wear loincloths?
ARMAND
I've never been there. . . .
IRMA
What an unimaginable negro!

ARMAND

I've never had any desire to leave Paris. I speak only French.

[Roussel 1994, pp. 86–87, ll. 758–66]

This exchange illustrates what Patrick Besnier, in his preface to *La Seine*, calls "the disturbance and the seduction" of Africa in Roussel's work (Roussel 1994, 23). But although Africa is certainly a privileged site of fantasy, Roussel's exoticism encompassed other colonial locales as well. The dilemmas and redefinitions brought about by contact between cultures—in particular, between colonizing and colonized cultures—resurface in Roussel's later plays. In *L'Étoile au front*, twinning and *métissage* (hybridity) become alternative models of cultural contact: twinning is an image of assimilation, or the transformation of the colonies into little replicas of France which, when taken together, make up *la plus grande France;* and *métissage* (in a reversal of its function at the 1937 World's Fair) is an image of association, a hybrid of French and indigenous cultures that adopt certain French ways while retaining enough of the native customs to remain recognizably different. In *La Poussière de soleils*, the difference that establishes identity takes on a diachronic dimension: the notion of modernity is bound up with the "discovery" of an antithetical, historical "other." The notion of the primitive expresses the desired dichotomy between "us" and "them" in terms of "now" and "then."

L'ÉTOILE AU FRONT

Before closing after only a three-day run in May 1925, Raymond Roussel's play *L'Étoile au front* (henceforth *Étoile*) provoked a maelstrom of public and critical outrage (Ferry 1953, 177–211; Caradec 1972, 227–75). The uproar was so great that the police were called in during one performance to evacuate the Vaudeville theater. Reviews of the play were devoted primarily to condemning the actors who had agreed to perform in it and accusing them of selling out for the enormous sums paid them by the author. There was even an editorial debate sparked by the question, "Is it an artist's duty to turn down certain roles?" (Ferry 1953, 193). Roussel's only supporters seem to have been a handful of Surrealists, who attacked members of the audience who had insulted the actors on stage.[3] *Étoile* has perhaps generated more indignation than any other work in the idiosyncratic author's unconventional oeuvre.

What so enraged audiences about the play was its absence of a plot (see Matthews 1966, 15; and Caradec 1972, 239). As one reviewer put it, "Nothing happens; there is no plot, not even an inane one" (cited in Ferry 1953, 190). *L'Étoile au front* consists entirely of a series of anecdotes and stories exchanged between two rare book collectors and their families about recent acquisitions. (A spectator at one performance is said to have yelled with mock enthusiasm at the end of each story: "Let's hear another one!" [Caradec 1972, 247].) Roussel reveals the meaning of the play's title only in the last scene: "l'étoile au front" is the sign (figured as a birthmark on the forehead) that has marked creative genius throughout the ages, a theme that recurs in many of the stories and, apparently, pertains to Roussel himself, by virtue of his prodigious storytelling abilities. The stories are not staged or dramatized in any way; they are simply told. Even Roussel referred to *Étoile* as a "livre" (1995, 11 and 25), although it was written for the stage, unlike *Impressions d'Afrique* and *Locus Solus*, novels that were eventually adapted for the theater. In *Étoile*, characters take turns narrating and listening—or, as is often the case, both at once, as questions asked by interlocutors usually serve to advance the narrative. The stories are more often than not embedded within other stories, as many as five times over: the first anecdote, for example, comprises a story-within-a-story-within-a-story-within-a-story-within-a-story (Roussel 1963a, 14–22). The stories or sets of stories are usually triggered by an object, but they are occasionally prompted by an association with a preceding story. Were it not for the twelve characters who tell the stories, the work would resemble more a dialogue in the tradition of Plato and Diderot than a play.

The only action that could possibly be said to resemble a plot occurs in the first act, when it is announced that the Indian twins who have been adopted and brought back from Pondicherry by one of the book collectors (Trézel) are in danger of being kidnapped, having been designated sacrificial victims by an Indian priest. The kidnapping is averted when Trézel's French-Indian maid, Meljah, also from Pondicherry, agrees to elope with the man sent to kidnap the twins. By the second act, however, this story line has played itself out and the twin girls are never mentioned again. (During the second act, a member of the audience is said to have cried: "What about the twins? I want to see the twins!" [Caradec 1972, 245].)

Despite the disappearance of the story line, however, the themes introduced in this protoplot resonate throughout the play. The Indian girls and the French-Indian woman may disappear as characters with the aborted plot, but the abstract figures that represent—Twins and the

Métis(se) [hybrid]—recur frequently in the stories the other characters (and, before their disappearance, they themselves) tell. These stories involve situations in which differences among individuals are effaced in order to establish homogeneous groups that are then opposed to one another. The effacement of difference among individuals is predicated on the creation of an aestheticized "type" that is superimposed on each member of a group; by means of this superimposition, difference is pushed outside, to be invoked between or among groups rather than within them. In the context of this displacement of difference, it is no accident that an impending sacrifice binds the fate of the twins to that of the "hybrid" woman in Roussel's play. Sacrifice eliminates in order to preserve on another level: in the case of stereotype, difference itself is eliminated, only to be resurrected with renewed strength.

The alliance between identity and difference illustrated thematically in *L'Étoile au front* is reinforced by the play's formal conceit: it is one of the works Roussel wrote using the *procédé*, the linguistic trick he revealed in his posthumously published book-length essay *Comment j'ai écrit certains de mes livres*, written shortly before his death in 1932. According to Roussel, the *procédé* involves the selection of two sentences (or phrases) that, when uttered, sound nearly identical, differing only by a single phoneme. The first example Roussel provides of his *procédé* has become the most illustrious: "I would choose two almost identical words (in the manner of metagrams)—for example, 'billard' and 'pillard.' Then I would add words that, while similar, had two different meanings, thereby obtaining two almost identical phrases" (Roussel 1995, 11). The two *almost* identical phrases in question—"Les lettres du blanc sur les bandes du vieux billard" [The white letters on the border of the old billiard table] and "Les lettres du blanc sur les bandes du vieux pillard" [The white man's letters about the old pillager's hordes]—were used to begin and end a story entitled "Parmi les noirs" (Among the Blacks), which was eventually expanded, the author tells us, to become the novel *Impressions d'Afrique*. The four hundred–plus pages of Roussel's best-known novel were thus conceived in the linguistic space between *b* and *p*—as well as in the cultural space between the "white man" of the trick sentence and the "blacks" of the story's title.

Julia Kristeva has described Roussel's *procédé* as the "pairing of words according to their phonetic resemblance, and filling of the semantic gap thus created, by a 'story'" (1978, 173). This "resemblance" acquires meaning only in relation to the play of difference that engenders a semiotic system.[4] The imbrication of resemblance and difference enacted by the *procédé* is mirrored in the figures of hybridity and twinning that circulate throughout *Étoile*. A figure like the *métis(se)* presupposes a difference whose collapse hybridity represents: in order to conceptualize the *métis(se)*, one must be able to conceptualize a distinct group represented by each of its halves. Yet the construction of mutually exclusive groups itself presupposes a multiplication or interchangeability of the singular within each group analogous to that represented in *Étoile*'s images of twins.

It is not accidental that the play's most symbolically important characters are colonial subjects: the identification of difference and the loss of diversity it entails are the major functions of colonial discourse. The colonized status of the twins and Meljah foregrounds the social and political implications of the identification of difference. In order to grasp these implications, it is first necessary to consider in their own right the symbolic roles of the hybrid and of twins in the play.

Métis(se)

The epistemological dilemma posed by hybridization is dramatized in *L'Étoile au front* by the French-Indian woman named Meljah, brought back from Pondicherry by the book collector Trézel to work as his maid. When her childhood sweetheart arrives from India to collect the twins designated for sacrifice, Meljah is torn between the conflicting value systems of her double heritage: "My French heritage tells me to turn you in; my Indian heritage approves of your action; that which one half of me sees as a crime, the other views as a necessary and legitimate human sacrifice" (1.5.60). *L'Étoile au front* presents conflicting images (or rather, a single hybrid image) of *métissage*, as if it were enacting the very doubleness it represents: on the one hand, the possibility of being both French and Indian is foreclosed, as Meljah is forced to choose one culture to the exclusion of another; but on the other hand, her final decision to return to India, predicated on preserving the Indian twins from sacrifice, is a concession to French ethical norms. Meljah thus manages to identify with both cultures at the very moment that she must define herself in opposition to one of them. Yet, precisely because the two cultures are presented in opposition to one another, her refusal to reject either one precludes her acceptance by its rival. Unable to identify completely with either group, Meljah is doomed to exclusion by both.

The cultural dilemma associated with *métissage* is reinforced in a story about a bas-relief that Geneviève, Trézel's niece, gives Meljah in an effort to inspire her to convert to Christianity. The bas-relief depicts a woman of French-Indian origin who, like Meljah, has difficulty choosing between the two cultures. The woman, Ghulkir, is won over to Christianity when she is able, miraculously, to tame a wild panther. Ghulkir subsequently joins a convent that imposes a "strict isolation" (1.5.63), where her pious devotion makes her a legend. This legend, recounted by Meljah, clearly fails to achieve the desired effect—"It was for my benefit that [Geneviève] bought and displayed this bas-relief by Carpeaux, explaining at length the story behind it" (1.5.60)—because Meljah, unlike her inspirational model, ultimately rejects Christianity. Ghulkir's *decision*, as the word's etymology (*de-caedere*) suggests, cuts her off entirely from Indian culture (and most of French culture), resulting in her confinement within the convent: "Each member of the convent is literally confined for life" (1.5.63). Her decision to convert to Christianity is the last she will ever be at liberty to make. Perhaps, then, Ghulkir's assimilation into French culture is not so different from Meljah's rejection of it: isolation or seclusion within a culture is also a form of exclusion from it. In both cases, cultural assimilation is problematic.

Étoile's stories of attempted—and failed—assimilation serve to underscore the differences between those trying to assimilate and the groups from which they are excluded. In one such story, an artist, Alfred Magdalou, suspects that his brother, Octave, is illegitimate and thus not entitled to share the inheritance Alfred is to receive when his father dies. With his artist's eye for anatomy, Alfred notices in his brother an "exoticism of the physique" (3.2.168) and travels to Peru to research the family tree of Enrique, the man with whom his mother, he suspects, had an affair. There he comes across a portrait, painted on a menu, of Enrique's grandmother posing suggestively with a man of African descent, referred to as a "negro don Juan" (3.2.171). This is just the proof Alfred needs to contest Octave's claim to the inheritance. In order to protect himself in case he were to lose this evidence, Alfred paints a copy of the portrait menu, which is certified as an exact reproduction of the original. It is the copy that ends up in an antique shop in Paris, coveted by art collectors as the earliest known work to use a color called "bleu Thénard."

The painting, which bears witness to the origin of a color, prompts the story about a color of origin. The birth that the painting reveals is marked by an indelible difference, which makes assimilation impossible. Not only is art used to identify—by identifying with—difference (the painting's testimonial value rests on its mimetic relationship to its subject, the black man), but it is Alfred's artistic background that enables

him to identify the difference that will exclude his brother from the line
of inheritance:

GASTON
... sculpting had even led him to dabble in anatomy. ...

JOUSSAC
... so useful to the disciples of Phidias.

GASTON
His knowledge of this science had caused him to notice that the angular
shape of his brother's face was the unmistakable sign of close Negro ancestry. (3.2.169).

In this exchange, "science" and aesthetics combine to underwrite the
ethnological doctrines of Gobineau and Alexis Carrel (Gobineau 1970;
Carrel 1968). The anecdote illustrates the stereotypes that result when
someone designated "different" is identified with an aesthetic representation—which is used as a model for classifying other examples of a
"type." Such identifications invariably result in the establishment of a
dichotomy between identifier(s) and identified, a dichotomy that in this
case serves to exclude the latter from an economic privilege accorded the
former.

Another anecdote in the play to incorporate the figure of the hybrid at
first glance seems to illustrate the possibility of cultural synthesis but actually forecloses that possibility. The story's thematization of difference
is foregrounded by Trézel, who discovers that the seemingly repetitive
lyrics of a traditional Hindi song sung by the Indian twins can in fact be
differentiated from one another: "Although I am unfamiliar with the
Hindi language, by paying attention to certain words whose physiog-
nomy had appealed to me, it seemed to me that although the music was
based on repetition, the lyrics not only changed ceaselessly but differed
each time I heard the song." The song's lyrics tell of the ancient republic
of Lirtossovie, situated on the border of Russia and India and plagued
by a "perpetual conflict between specimens of two races too different
from one another" (1.4.39). Each group retains its own customs, entirely
separate from the other: "In this part of the world, everything was
double: language, religion, clothing." The dissension continues until the
election of a leader named Houril, who is perfectly suited to represent
both factions equally: "His dual Russian-Indian ancestry could be seen
in his eyes, one of which, a Nordic blue, contrasted with the other, a
deep, tropical black" (1.4.40). The citizens of the republic find peace for

the first time through their newly elected representative, whose perfect impartiality "resulted from the equal division, indicated by the disparity of his eyes, that made his soul both Russian and Indian" (1.4.41). This anecdote would seem to provide an illustration of a successful synthesis. The elected official's appearance, however, rather than eradicate difference, emphasizes it; he is the incarnation of doubleness, not of unity. Hybridity is shown here to resolve differences but not to efface them. This is because the construction of the figure of the hybrid itself is grounded in the concept of mutually exclusive racial categories, without which it would not be distinguishable from other identities.

Only one anecdote in *Étoile* provides an illustration of unproblematized assimilation, serving as a counterexample to the Lirtossovie story. The contrasting anecdote describes the plot of an opera set in pre-Columbian North America, in which two young lovers, forced to meet clandestinely because they come from warring tribes, become stranded on an island when a storm blows their boats away. The two tribes set aside their differences and forge a tunnel beneath the water that will lead them to the island. In the course of the rescue, "the two rival tribes [*tribus*] naturally became indistinguishable," the collaboration resulting in a "détente soon followed by fraternization" (3.4.209). This story contains the play's most explicit depiction of the eradication of difference—which, as a result, marks the story's absolute difference within the play. The fact that the differences between the tribes are effaced so easily suggests that their distinguishing features are more arbitrary, less essential, than those invoked between groups in the play's tales of racial difference.

The resolution of difference between the tribes is tantamount to its extinction and requires nothing more than the presence of both parties in the same place at the same time. The simplicity of this solution implies that the North American indigenous cultures are less complicated than those of the rival factions in Lirtossovie. The word "tribu" adds to the aura of primitiveness, distancing the Amerindians further from the Lirtossovians. On hearing the story of the tiny Indo-Russian republic, Trézel mentions having read about it in a book, written by a sociologist, called *La Filiation des coutumes*: "This is one of a thousand examples he invokes in order to link all rites the world over, past and present" (1.4.43–44). The other characters in the play, as well as the audience, are thus meant to identify with the Lirtossovians. Such identification, however, is not encouraged with the Amerindian tribes; on the contrary, the simplicity of the latter, their facile resolution of differences, opposes them not only to the Lirtossovians but to everyone else as well. Difference, once operative between the tribes, is invoked to define the relationship between, on the one hand, both tribes united, and, on the other hand, the play's speakers (and its audience). The Amerindian anecdote thus enacts the identification of difference.

The contrast between the two stories considered above is grounded in their differing conceptualization of boundaries. In the story of Lirtossovie, boundaries are crossed but ultimately maintained (indeed, their transgression only reinforces them). In the tale of the rival Amerindian tribes, the boundary between groups is dissolved—only to be reestablished between, on the one hand, the subjects of the *énoncé* (both tribes lumped together as the subject of the story) and, on the other, the subjects of the *énonciation* (the storytellers). In the telling of this tale, difference is pushed outside one set of boundaries in order to create another.

Double Trouble

In the logic of Roussel's play, the figure of twins (one-in-two) represents an inversion of the figure of the hybrid (two-in-one). Two is the smallest possible plurality, the minimum number needed to create a system. It is no accident that Roussel's discussion of *L'Étoile au front* in *Comment j'ai écrit certains de mes livres* is based precisely (and entirely) on the question of the singular and the plural: "As I have said before, my two books *L' Étoile au front* and *La Poussière de soleils* are constructed according to this same method. Notably, I recall [*Je me rappelle notamment*] that in the Pope Jules episode in *L'Étoile au front*, the words 'singular' and 'plural' led to 'Saint Jules' and 'wrap' (*pelure*). (In fact, among my papers there can be found a very clear explanation of how I wrote *L'Étoile au front* and *La Poussière de soleils*. . . .)" (Roussel 1995, 25).

Needless to say, the proposed "very clear explanation" has yet to be found. Roussel's readers are left with this single and singular example, noted from memory and remembered notably ("Je me rappelle notamment"). It is the only mention Roussel makes of the play, apart from his parenthetical citation of it in the essay's opening sentence: "I had always planned to explain how I wrote certain books . . . (*Impressions d'Afrique, Locus Solus, L'Étoile au front*, and *La Poussière de soleils*)" (1995, 11). The Pope Jules anecdote is the only example Roussel remembers, or claims to remember.

The episode singled out by Roussel for posterity is narrated in the play's second act. While pausing to admire a life-sized nativity scene in the papal gardens, Pope (Saint) Jules sees a shivering child, and on learning that the boy has been praying for nothing more than a "pelure" (wrap) to keep from catching cold, lets him take a blanket from the crèche. The pope, hoping to make an example of the child's piety, "wished to mark [*illustrer*], by means of some special reward, conduct that bespoke such profound devotion and piety." The double meaning of the word "illustrer"—to make illustrious and to illustrate—is emphasized when it is added that the child's conduct was rewarded "so that, praised by all, it would be imitated by many" (2.4.98). This exemplary illustration of an illustrious example insists on the iterability of the singular, its potential for proliferation. In the middle of all this mimetic multiplication is Christ, source of inspiration for both the child's prayer and the pope's good deed. As a hybrid—part god, part human—Christ embodies the passage from plural to singular; as a teacher, he commandeers the didactic transformation from singular to plural by inciting others to follow his example. As a sacrificial victim, Christ evokes the plight of the Indian twins, raising the question of ritual violence.

The implications of Roussel's treatment of this subject can best be illuminated by examining it in light of a classic theory of ritual violence, that developed by René Girard. In *The Violence and the Sacred* (1977), Girard contends that sacrifice is "an instrument of prevention in the struggle against violence" (17). A sacrificial crisis results from nondifferentiation: "Wherever differences are lacking, violence threatens" (57). Girard describes this "crisis of distinctions" (52) as "the dissolution of regulations pertaining to the individual's proper place in society" (56). For Girard, difference is inseparable from hierarchy, which provides the foundation for social harmony.

In order to illustrate nondifferentiation, Girard invokes the image of twins, which "offer[s] a symbolic representation, sometimes remarkably eloquent, of the symmetrical conflict and identity crisis that characterize the sacrificial crisis" (62–63). Girard, perceiving identity in the rivalries that abound in classical tragedy, sees the image of twins in seeming opposites, whose conflict is based on a mutual desire or goal. In *L'Étoile au front*, such a rivalry occurs between Trézel and Joussac, both collectors of rare books. Throughout the play, each tries to outdo the other by acquiring the most precious edition of a book, manuscript, or work of art. The rivalry is good-natured, but it is a rivalry nonetheless: when Trézel is able to come up with a filigreed manuscript that predates a manuscript in Joussac's possession previously thought to be the first of its kind,

Joussac whimpers, "Now my little monogram has lost all its value. . . . How humiliating!" (3.2.201).

For Girard, twins are the symbol par excellence of nondifferentiation. The force of this symbol is such that it affects everything and everyone, proliferating until whole communities are transformed in its image:

> The antagonists caught up in the sacrificial crisis invariably believe themselves to be separated by insurmountable differences. In reality, however, these differences gradually wear away. Everywhere we now encounter the same desire, the same antagonism, the same strategies—the same illusion of rigid differentiation within a pattern of ever-expanding uniformity. As the crisis grows more acute, the community members are transformed into "twins," matching images of violence. I would be tempted to say that they are each *doubles* of one another. (78–79; original emphasis)

Twinness is contagious; the pluralization process is not limited to the doubling of a single entity but continues, multiplying pluralities. Girard even sees twins where there are none, as when he refers to Freud's description of the chorus in a Greek tragedy as a "foule des doubles" (Girard 1972, 297), citing a passage from *Totem and Taboo* in which Freud actually speaks of "Eine Schar von Personen," or crowd of *people*, in the German (Freud 1978, 187).[5] The fact that nowhere in the passage Girard cites does Freud mention twins or doubling does not deter Girard from transforming the Greek chorus into a troupe of twins. From Freud's individuals to Girard's doubles, the distance is exactly as great as that between the throng of doubles and the sacrificial victim that stands in for them all:

> If violence is a great leveler of men and everybody becomes the double, or "twin," of his antagonist, it seems to follow that all the doubles are identical and that any one can at any given moment become the double of all the others; that is, the sole object of universal obsession and hatred. A single victim can be substituted for all the potential victims, for all the enemy brothers that each member is striving to banish from the community; he can be substituted for each and every member of the community. (Girard 1977, 79)

The distinguishing feature of such a victim is precisely its lack of distinguishing features; he or she must be able to fit all identities, like a master key. This absolute interchangeability represents the ultimate state of nondifferentiation, or what Girard calls "violent unanimity" (1977, 78). Girard then distinguishes between two kinds of violence: generative and ritual. Generative violence refers to a specific event said to have taken place in the past (like the primal murder in *Totem and Taboo*). Ritual violence, in contrast, is the repetition of generative violence on a symbolic level. The violence of this act is directed toward victims who come from outside the community. In this ritual form of violence, when members of a group are entirely interchangeable with one another and with the victim chosen to represent them, one final substitution takes place. Girard argues that "all sacrificial rites are based on two substitutions. The first is provided by generative violence, which substitutes a single victim for all the members of the community. The second, the only strictly ritualistic substitution, is that of a victim for the surrogate victim. As we know, it is essential that the victim be drawn from outside the community. The surrogate victim, by contrast, is a member of the community" (269). Although Girard specifies here that victims must come from "outside the community," elsewhere he revises this requirement: the victim "should belong both inside and outside the community" (272). The contradiction is only apparent, because the source of the violence lies neither outside the community nor both inside *and* outside the community; rather, it lies in the very distinction between inside and outside that a collective identity makes possible.

Girard emphasizes that the victim of a ritual sacrifice must be chosen arbitrarily, but at the same time, he or she must meet certain qualifications. The seemingly incompatible requirements of arbitrariness and motivation can both be met only if the victim is selected at random from a preordained class of victim. Girard is thus able to speak of "sacrificeable categories," which differ from community to community. The value of this theory consists in its insight about the establishment of an oppressed class and a corresponding oppressor class. In the context of violent unanimity, the scapegoating of individuals is always already the scapegoating of groups. In Girard's analysis, however, plurality is dismissed—one might say sacrificed—in favor of singularity. Both the transformation of Freud's *Personen* into "doubles" and the latter's subsequent proliferation are grounded in the assumption that all people in a given group are interchangeable, that plurality is synonymous with homogeneity. Girard moves from one to two in order, ultimately, to be able to move back to one again, to a unity which incorporates all doubles—

and which effaces, moreover, the difference between two *kinds* of twins, not all of which (nor of whom) are identical.

The positing of difference on one level is always accompanied by its effacement on another level: in *Étoile*, the subjects of failed assimilation can be marked as different because they are posited as "types," identified (and thus rendered interchangeable) with other members of their designated group. Likewise, Girard notes that it is twins' sameness that differentiates them from others: "In the case of twins, symmetry and identity are represented in extraordinarily explicit terms; nondifference is present in concrete, literal form, but this form is itself so exceptional as to constitute a new difference. Thus the *representation* of nondifference ultimately becomes the very exemplar of difference" (64).

Such, then, is the meaning of the play's sublimated sacrifice: the Indian twins may be spirited away, out of harm's reach, but the difference whose effacement they represent does not escape immolation.

The Forces of Reproduction

Two of the stories told in *L'Étoile au front* provide a stark illustration of the sacrifice of difference that enables the construction of stereotype. In the first of the stories, which are told back to back, a wealthy French plantation owner in New Caledonia forms a league to combat the proliferation of an insect that is rapidly destroying the island's crops. An emblem is chosen to represent the group:

MADAME JOUSSAC
Every league needs an insignia. Masclet selected for his league a female specimen of the insect, with horribly swelled womb, half hidden by a dele.
TRÉZEL
What better way to sum up the league's goal of destruction, and the dangerous reproductive potential of its enemy? (2.3.180–81)

This peculiarly misogynistic tale is the only story told by the only mother in the play's cast of characters. The flag's freakish depiction of fecundity and the squeamish voyeurism it elicits are paralleled in the story that follows, which takes place in French Guyana in 1692. Frontin, the French valet of a wealthy Creole nobleman, impregnates a slave of African descent, who escapes with the valet's money and hides in the forest. The valet finally succeeds in locating the woman, through the supernatural intervention of the ghost of Meleager, one of Jason's Argonauts, whom the valet is to portray in a "grand historical parade" (3.3.192) in celebration of the two hundredth anniversary of Columbus's arrival in the New World. The ghost leads the valet deep into the forest so that he may observe the slave woman, who does not know she is being watched, with "four newborn mulattos [*mulâtres*]" (194). The nervous jokes exchanged among character-narrators after this disclosure reveal a discomfort with fertility similar to that displayed in the anti-insect emblem of the previous anecdote:

TRÉZEL
Four! Poor Frontin . . .
JOUSSAC
Hidden off to the left, he watches from behind the vines, making bitterly comical remarks to his guide . . .
CLAUDE
. . . inspired by the sight of the four twins he's authored!
TRÉZEL
A veritable litter!
JOUSSAC
He stood there, dumbfounded, for a long time . . .
CLAUDE
Troubled by the sight of his treasure in such company! (3.3.195; original ellipses)

In this passage, the slave woman is made the repository of the "dangerous reproductive potential" previously attributed to the Caledonian insects. Like the insects that threaten to overrun a colony and make it uninhabitable for the colonists, the slave's babies represent uncontrollable fecundity, the possible proliferation of colonized subjects, which would pose a threat to French colonists. Yet no such threat ever existed historically, nor was one perceived: both French Guyana and New Caledonia were always sparsely populated in the colonial period, a fact that colonial historians lamented (Vallin 1987, 40–41 and 55). The fear of fecundity expressed in this passage must be understood differently. There is no question that the infants' status as twinned twins ("les quatre jumeaux") evokes the proliferative power of twins that Girard speaks of. But these infants are also "mulâtres," and as such, they incorporate, in a single image, the play's dual figures of twins and the hybrid.

The fact that the infants are described as twins emphasizes their status as a symbol of nondifferentiation; the fact that they are described as "mulâtres" points to their status as representatives of the excluded. The combination illustrates the complicity of exclusion and stereotype with a violence similar to that of the dele that adorns the colonizer's bug-repellent flag. The biological reproduction thematized in the two anecdotes provides a starkly literal image of the reproduction of colonial relations. Yet, the difference posited between the parents of the quadruplets is not so great that they cannot procreate, a possibility that would be precluded if they belonged to different species: in this sense, the difference between them is minimal, like that between "billard" and "pillard" in Roussel's *procédé*. The profusion and homogeneity of the couple's offspring thus bear witness to the marriage of identity and difference celebrated throughout the play, and to the slavish stereotypes this union engenders. *L'Étoile au front* shows that group identities are born at the crossroads of semiotics and politics, suggesting that the sacrifice of difference begins—but does not end—with language.

LA POUSSIÈRE DE SOLEILS

The "discovery" of hidden differences thematized in *L'Étoile au front* is expressed as the discovery of a hidden past in Roussel's second play, which highlights the convergence of synchronic boundaries and diachronic divisions.

La Poussière de soleils represented a concession to audiences who had derided Roussel's first theatrical endeavor because it lacked a discernible plot. According to critics, however, *La Poussière de soleils* had the opposite problem: it suffered from a hyperactive plot. The play's dizzying pace made it nearly impossible to follow the chain of events; in some cases, characters spend only a few seconds on stage between elaborate scene changes. One critic observed in the February 5, 1926, issue of *Le Matin* that "the short episodes are divided up like little vignettes. The curtain lowers before scenes appear to have ended and is only raised again after the orchestra has emitted an assortment of false notes and various other noises" (cited in Caradec 1972, 293). The impression of rapid change the play conveyed intrigued spectators and critics, who felt that it must harbor some hidden significance.

There has been much speculation that this hyperbolic rapidity must have been intended to focus attention on the *number* of scene changes, to which Roussel enthusiasts attributed an alchemical significance. The most famous proponent of this theory was André Breton, who, in his preface to Jean Ferry's 1953 study of Roussel, contends that *Poussière* is full of occult symbols (reprinted in Breton 1967, 237). Marcel Jean and Arpad Mezei's *Genèse de la pensée moderne*, published in 1950, also advanced this hypothesis, claiming that the play "is constructed around the number 24, with 24 scenes and 24 characters. . . . Thanks to the presentation of scenes, the general concept of astronomical measurement can be clearly discerned. Following a twelve-part rhythm, the protagonists advance like planets through the chronological procession of signs of the zodiac constituted by the various narratives" (197–98). Such speculation was soon repudiated by Roussel's friend Michel Leiris and by Jean Ferry himself, who, in 1965, declared Breton's preface to his study of Roussel to be "monumental garbage" (Brotchie, Green et al. 1987, 80 and 106).

For those engaged in the debate, the play's emphasis on change signaled that there was a discovery to be made. What Breton and company failed to realize, however, was that the discovery the play invites is, as Sjef Houppermans points out, that of discovery itself: "The occult, obscure, and cabalistic images function less as keys than as clues announcing merely the existence of a secret" (1985, 180). Roussel added to the air of mystery in *Comment j'ai écrit certain de mes livres* when he announced that *Poussière* was one of the four works he wrote using the *procédé*. Yet this work has the distinction of being the only one from which Roussel did not cite any examples of the *procédé*—as we have seen, even *L'Étoile au front* was good for one example. As far as the *procédé* is concerned, then, *Poussière* remains shrouded in secrecy. By casting his second and last play in the framework of discovery within which the play itself operates, Roussel was in effect announcing the existence of a hidden treasure, without providing any maps or clues. The fact that the play's rapid changes suggested to critics that something was hidden, something to be discovered, underscores the association between change and discovery in the modern imagination. Indeed, discovery, credited with inaugurating change, is implicit in the very notion of modernity.

The play's setting, French Guyana, grounds the discourse of discovery in a specifically colonial context. Colonial expansion in the industrial era and the attendant anthropological enterprise have defined modernity in terms of synchronic, as well as diachronic, difference—the distinction between "now" and "then" has become inseparable from the distinction between "us" and "them." Jacques Le Goff has noted the change in priorities that comes with modern imperialism: what was formerly "ancient" becomes "primitive" (1988, 94). The new conception of the primitive combines spatial and temporal alterity, suggesting that people who live in certain parts of the world are the products of another age. Johannes Fabian names this attribution of a different temporality to dominated cultures the "denial of coevalness" (1993, 31), which is a function of what he calls "allochronism" (32).

By opposing its linear sense of time to the cyclical one it attributes to "primitive" societies, a self-proclaimed modern society can confirm its impression of its own rapid change. In order to do this, modernity must project a vision of an other that is eternally self-present, unchanging— blissfully ignorant, in other words, of the loss with which modernity itself is obsessed. For it is in terms of loss that modernity conceives history, building monuments to act as surrogates for what has been lost. This monumental sense of mourning pervades *La Poussière de soleils*.

Columbus's Precursor

When *Poussière* opens, Guillaume Blache, a wealthy colonial landowner and entrepreneur, has just died. His nephew and sole heir, Julien Blache, has come to French Guyana to claim his inheritance, only to learn that Guillaume, in the grip of an "incurable misanthropy" (1.1.10) following the death of his wife and child in an epidemic, converted his entire fortune into precious gems, which he hid to prevent others from profiting from it (1.1.11). The elaborate game of hide-and-seek that ensues foregrounds the play's emphasis on discovery. *Poussière*, like *Comment j'ai écrit certains de mes livres*, begins with a posthumous revelation; namely, that shortly before his death, Guillaume Blache, troubled by "eleventh-hour remorse stemming from the heinous action attributed to him" (1.5.21), left a series of elaborately obscure clues to facilitate the recovery of the jewels.[6]

One revelation leads to another. As Julien Blache explains at the end of the play, when the treasure has been found, along with a confession written by his uncle:

> He made sure that there was a path leading to the treasure, whose existence would calm his misgivings—and whose intended difficulty, increased by thousands of traps, would appease his misanthropy. . . . But, as the beginning of the path, which has no discernible sign, would be especially difficult to find, his conscience dictated that there be at least one additional way in. So he created two starting points. (5.8.194)[7]

The second trail of clues is followed by a trio of professional thieves, quintessential bad guys who play opposite the team of good guys led by Julien Blache.

A preoccupation with discovery also informs the play's romantic subplot, in which Julien's daughter, the uniquely angelic Solange, falls in love with Jacques, a foundling who is searching for his roots. Jacques insists on keeping their engagement secret because he is afraid Solange's father would not allow her to marry a "modest legal scribe" (1.7.40). While Solange's father tries to recover the inheritance that will one day belong to Solange, Jacques embarks on a parallel search for the pedigree that will make him a suitable husband to an heiress. In a scene emblematic of the play's theme of discovery, the lovers come upon a monument commemorating an ancient Iberian woman named Saenca, sole survivor of a shipwreck that washed her up on the shores of Sinnamarie long before Columbus's arrival in the New World and who committed suicide rather than endure separation from her fiancé at home. Close scrutiny of this scene reveals (to use the language of discovery) the alliance between discovery and loss in colonial discourse.

There are actually four discoveries recounted in the scene, which is situated exactly halfway through the play. The first, in chronological but not narrative order, is Saenca's "discovery" of the American continent: she is billed as "an authentic precursor of Columbus" (2.12.103). Saenca is then herself "discovered" by the local inhabitants, the Élékéiks. The chronology then skips ahead several centuries to the discovery of the legend's existence by French colonists. Finally (but this is presented first in the narrative), the whole legend is "discovered" by Solange, to whom Jacques shows the statue of Saenca erected by the colonists at the site of her suicide.

Of these four discoveries, one is notable for the contrast it draws between two cultures: "A rock on which Saenca had engraved a short, dated confession addressed to her fiancé was found [*trouvée*] by the area's first colonists in the hands of the [*aux mains des*] Élékéiks, who later told them the story of her dramatic suicide, which had been handed down to them in a striking tradition" (2.12.102). As this passage illustrates, the "discovery" made by the colonists is actually an expropriation: the word "trouvée" strips the Élékéiks of their possessive agency, rendering them passive objects, and the fact that the confession is first "aux mains des" Élékéiks reveals that it was "taken" rather than "found." The expression "aux mains des," which implies that the Élékéiks have stolen the confession, further suggests that the expropriation is morally justified and that the colonists, not the Élékéiks, are the rightful heirs to Saenca's legacy. Saenca and the French colonists are connected, across a great temporal divide, in an alliance that excludes the Élékéiks. This alliance is based on a shared mode of commemoration that opposes the Europeans to the inhabitants of the New World.

The Élékéiks' tradition is clearly an oral one, embodied in the story handed down to them from their ancient forebears. The implication is that the legend remains unchanged while in their possession—preserved like one of the relics that will remain intact until its seizure by colonists: "The Élékéiks soon found among the rocks what remained of an ivory statuette, which they preserved, having seen Saenca use it religiously. Eager to utilize this relic, the authors of the statue you see before you carved this ivory stylus, which couples who are about to marry use during their traditional visit to engrave commemorative thoughts, names, and dates in the base of the statue" (2.12.103). The colonists are linked to Saenca by the fact that their commemorative practices involve writing. It is significant that the word Solange uses to describe Saenca's suicide connotes, among other things, writing: "The deed [*trait*] warranted dignified commemoration" (2.12.102). But despite this common bond, despite the fact that the statue in which people inscribe dated "commemorative thoughts" replicates Saenca's own confession, inscribed in a rock and dated, the colonists and Saenca are more strongly linked by their status as agents of discovery and thus of change. The discourse of discovery implies a passive object—here the Élékéiks, fixed in an unchanging tradition. The passage cited above in which the colonists recast Saenca's statuette into a stylus succinctly presents the terms of the contrast: what the Élékéiks preserve intact throughout the centuries the colonists are "eager to utilize," that is, appropriate and transform so as to make unrecognizable. In this respect, the passage resembles the one in which the colonists find Saenca's confession "aux mains des" Élékéiks: in both cases, the Élékéiks are portrayed merely as caretakers of a history from which they are excluded. By describing a passage from conservation to commemoration, or from the preservation of the past to the recognition of its loss, this scene imposes a dichotomy between Élékéik and European culture, between immutability and change. This sense of the natives' immutability is reinforced in an earlier scene:

BLACHE

The Élékéiks are ruled by a duumvirat?

BULUXIR

. . . just as their ancestors lived from time immemorial. . . . As they did in the beginning, they still periodically engrave the names of all their leaders, in twin lists on solid marble chosen expressly so as to prevent the alteration of what is carved on it. (1.5.28)

The fact that the Élékéiks' is a literate culture suggests that their contrast with the Europeans is not based on writing. Unlike the colonists, whose monuments and inscriptions bear witness to loss in the face of unremitting change, the Élékéiks' commemoration emphasizes their own sense of cultural continuity. The Élékéiks' written commemoration of their leaders is just as permanent as that of the Europeans, but in the context of a culture that lives "as their ancestors have lived from time immemorial," "since the dawn of time [*l'origine*]" (1.5.28), this permanence takes on a different meaning.

Writing, in other words, functions differently in different contexts. The inscription of the names of Élékéik rulers reflects the continuity of their culture, the monotonous regularity with which one ruler is replaced by another—but for the colonists, such commemorative practices serve to remind them of what they have lost, without offering any assurance that what is lost will be replaced. It is in this light that Jacques's refusal to carve "commemorative thoughts" in the statue of Saenca should be read, a refusal that would otherwise seem baffling, given his occupation as a legal scribe. The following exchange is provoked by Solange's suggestion that they, too, carve their names in the statue:

JACQUES

What good would it do? Won't we remember this wonderful moment without it?

SOLANGE

Oh, yes, forever!

JACQUES

In any case, I don't feel like writing on this stone today.

SOLANGE

Is that because you think these might be nothing but a collection of foolish quotations?

JACQUES

No, but wouldn't making a confession to this rock out in the open be tantamount to revealing the blessed secret that still surrounds our love? Instead, let's swear our eternal fidelity once more in the presence of Saenca, sublime fiancée.(1.12.104)

Jacques's reluctance to carve his name in the statue of Saenca displays what Jacques Derrida has called logocentrism, which devalues writing in favor of speech and presents it as a poor substitute for memory (Derrida 1976). In the logocentric tradition, writing at once effects and bears witness to a loss of memory. The Saenca scene, by evoking logocentrism, reveals that the nostalgia for oral culture so often expressed by ethnologists, and the nostalgia for unchanging societies so often expressed by historians, are based on similar assumptions about the societies one's own has "left behind." The very distinction between cultures whose commemorations are attempts to compensate for loss and those whose commemorative practices reinforce their temporal plenitude is a logocentric one. Such distinctions underlie conceptions of history that oppose a constantly changing modernity to a fossilized, archaic temporality.

The work of the historian Pierre Nora exemplifies this tendency to exoticize the past. In his general introduction to *Realms of Memory*, titled "Between Memory and History," Nora makes a distinction that relies on an opposition between the primitive and the modern, when he speaks of "the enormous distance that separates real memory—the kind of inviolate social memory that primitive and archaic societies embodied, and whose secret died with them—from history, which is how modern societies organize a past they are condemned to forget because they are driven by change" (1996, 2). This distinction coincides with logocentrism's nostalgia for an undifferentiated plenitude. Nora's use of the adjectives "real" (*vraie*) and "inviolate" (*intouchée*) evokes a prelapsarian golden age inhabited by noble savages. His depiction of modernity, however, is no less homogeneous, with "modern societies" (*nos sociétés*) swept up in a whirlwind of change as constant and unrelenting as the immobility that characterizes "primitive and archaic societies" (*les sociétés dites primitives*). These societies are the guardians of memory, "whose secret died with them"—a secret that it is the duty of the historian, ethnographer of the diachronic, to reveal.

According to this notion of history, to reveal a secret, or make a discovery, is to inaugurate loss. History, writes Nora, is the vain attempt to preserve a "passé définitivement mort" (which Nora's translator, Arthur Goldhammer, renders "an irretrievable past"; literally, Nora speaks of a past that is "definitively dead") (1). This attempt to invoke what is dead is a form of mourning. History must attempt to preserve memory because memory itself is a thing of the past: "Memory is constantly on our lips because it no longer exists" (1). But paradoxically, history destroys memory even as it attempts to preserve it: Nora speaks of an "uprooting of memory, its eradication by the conquering force of history" (2), for, he argues, the destruction of memory is ultimately history's "true mission" (3). What history preserves, then, is the loss of memory.

In *La Poussière de soleils*, history is embodied in the monuments erected to commemorate women and men who have died heroically. Indeed, the play could be called a monument to monuments. Among the monuments that commemorate those who have been lost, one commemorates loss itself: the statue of Saenca. As Jacques explains to Solange, "They turned her into a statue, giving her, without knowing what she actually looked like, the classic pose—perfect for an eternally abandoned fiancée—of the mourner with her head buried in her hands" (2.12.102–3). Jacques's refusal to consecrate the couple's visit to the statue by carving their names in it can thus be read as a desire to avoid being tainted by the loss that Saenca represents. Indeed, the separation between Saenca and her fiancé prefigures the temporary parting between Jacques and Solange at the end of the play, when Jacques reluctantly leaves for Rio on business. For Jacques, the statue is the vehicle for a kind of discovery that he hopes will not take place, because he fears that disclosure of the couple's engagement will lead to its cancellation. He does not want his "commemorative thoughts," in other words, to turn into a Saenca-like confession of lost love.

It is here that the meaning of the play's title becomes clear. Solange assures Jacques that, in his absence, "my image [*ma pensée*], in place of myself, will be with you always" (5.9.199). The "pensée" chosen to stand in for the absent lover is a "poussière de soleils," "an immense cloud of dust, composed of millions of particles, each of which is itself a sun situated in the center of a swirling planetary system."[8] It is Jacques who proposes the symbol of the multiple suns. In response to Solange's suggestion that they select a particular star or constellation, Jacques counters: "A star? a constellation? I have something better in mind" (5.9.199). Jacques's proposal names the *sol*eil that will stand in for *Sol*ange in her absence. Like the Medusa myth, which for Freud depicts the reassuring proliferation of an object threatened with loss (snakes = phallus) (see Freud 1981, 18:273–74), the profusion of suns peoples the sky with the lover Jacques fears losing. This star cluster will act as a surrogate presence, connecting the absent lovers to one another: "By focusing on it at the same time, we would forge something of a link between us"

(5.9.199). Houppermans has suggested that the image of the star cluster mirrors that of the hidden jewels (1985, 168). The celestial image, invoked after the recovery of the jewels, acts as a reassuring symbol at a time of impending loss. The treasure, once lost, has been found; by invoking an image that resembles it, the lovers are expressing the hope that their loss or separation is likewise reversible.

The *poussière de soleils*, then, is a personal monument of sorts, a surrogate for an absent beloved (despite its very public nature, up in the sky for all to see, the star cluster has value as a *symbol* only for Jacques and Solange). It is a monument that Jacques and Solange have created in order to preserve their own memory, the memory of their union. Two other personal monuments in the play share this narcissistic function. Like the *poussière de soleils* image, these monuments are self-made, but in a very literal sense.

Hysterical Landmarks

The first of these monuments, which provides the inaugural clue in the trail pursued by the thieves, is the skull of an Italian Renaissance poet, Ambrosi, "a young tubercular [who], certain to be taken by death before having achieved his first ray of glory, and counting little on posthumous fame, had found a way of at least saving his masterpiece, a sonnet, from oblivion by requesting in his will that it be engraved on his skull, in the center of the head that had created it" (1.6.36). This image, in which a poem is immortalized by its author (or its author's body), reverses the traditional conception of art, which is normally thought to immortalize the artist. Ambrosi's skull is evoked in the very next scene, when Jacques says to Solange, after repeating to her the agreed-on code for their clandestine meetings, "Those are your exact words, which I have engraved in my memory" (1.7.40). Ambrosi's synecdochical self-representation finds its parallel in Jacques's metaphor: like the dust of suns, Solange's words have become her metonymic replacement.

Another clue is explicitly linked to the first both syntagmatically, because it follows sequentially, and paradigmatically, because it, too, involves a work of art whose medium is a part of the body. This clue is found in a rare first edition of the novel *Manon Lescaut*, which apparently contains a scene in which the character Partelet presents Manon with a bust he has carved out of his amputated femur (recalling the character in *Impressions d'Afrique* who fashions a flute out of his own tibia [Roussel 1963b, 65–67]). This episode was supposedly cut (like the sculptor's leg) from all subsequent editions of *Manon Lescaut*.[9] Like Ambrosi, Partelet transforms a part of himself in order to remind someone from whom he must be separated of his absence. But the form this memento takes is, paradoxically, that of Manon herself: "During his convalescence, Partelet sculpted from memory a little bust of Manon out of his femur, in homage to her; it made him happy to think that this piece of himself would be lovingly treasured by the vain woman, because it glorified her beauty" (1.8.46). By appealing to Manon's narcissism, Partelet can ensure that part of him, at least, will never be separated from the object of his desire.

Despite their different aims—Ambrosi wishes to be remembered by as many people as possible, whereas Partelet has a specific person in mind—both anecdotes locate the human body as the repository of memory. It will be recalled that Freud, too, insisted on this function of the body, emphasizing that a patient's emotional history could be documented in his or her neurotic symptoms. In the "First Lecture on Psycho-Analysis," Freud explicitly compares hysterics' symptoms to monuments: "Their symptoms are residues and mnemic symbols of particular (traumatic) experiences. We may perhaps obtain a deeper understanding of this kind of symbolism if we compare them with other mnemic symbols in other fields. The monuments and memorials with which large cities are adorned are also mnemic symbols" (1989, 12). In the case study Freud uses to illustrate this lecture, the origin of the patient's symptoms is linked to the death of her father. The woman's loss finds expression in her body, in the hysterical symptoms for which she is treated. Symptoms are thus so many clues that can eventually lead the analyst to the buried memory at the origin of the affliction. Like the modernity that engendered it, Freudian psychoanalysis attributes a different temporality to its object; the unconscious, says Freud, is a mental function to which "the idea of time cannot be applied" (1967, 54). The psychoanalytic discourse of discovery, like its ethnographic and historiographic counterparts, comprises a quest for origins—origins that are never lost but that remain locked within the analysand, always ready to be relived under the analyst's watchful eye.

Throughout Roussel's work, anamnesis is shown to heal emotional wounds in scenes that mirror psychoanalytic sessions. In *Impressions d'Afrique*, the hypnotist Darriand restores Séil-kor's sanity by enabling him to relive the traumatic moments from childhood that resulted in the loss of his reason (Roussel 1963b, 152–63). In *Locus Solus*, Lucius

Egroïzard is cured of his melancholia when he hears a singer replicate the voice of his dead daughter (Roussel 1965, 221–41). Also in *Locus Solus*, thanks to Canterel's *résurrectine* and *vitalium*, wonder drugs that reanimate the dead for a few moments, a "young widow now alone in the world and plagued by thoughts of suicide deferred the execution of her tragic plans only in order to grant herself the cruel joy of seeing an artificial existence unstiffen the body of her son" (Roussel 1965, 171). As Houppermans puts it so succinctly, "Remembering, anamnesis, transference: Roussel's text is the generalization of this process" (1985, 277).

Roussel's depiction of anamnesis as a curative force is not unconnected to his allochronistic portrayal of the Élékéiks in *Poussière*. Like the Élékéiks' rites, the unconscious processes tapped in psychoanalysis were considered by Freud to exhibit an atemporal structure. As Freud writes in *Beyond the Pleasure Principle*, "We have learnt that unconscious mental processes are in themselves 'timeless' " (1967, 54). The ethnologists and historians who represent certain societies as changeless or atemporal do so at the risk of implying that these cultures (in contrast to their own) are dominated by unconscious drives, unrepressed, "natural," and hence uncivilized.[10] Nora (1996) can thus speak of "the distance between an integrated memory, all-powerful, sweeping, un-self-conscious, and inherently present-minded—a memory without a past that eternally recycles a heritage, relegating ancestral yesterdays to the undifferentiated time of heroes, inceptions, and myth—and our form of memory, which is nothing but history, a matter of sifting and sorting" (2).

In *La Poussière de soleils*, the contrast between the Élékéiks, living, it will be recalled, "as their ancestors had lived from time immemorial" (1.5.28), and the Europeans, preoccupied with commemorating their losses, is grounded in a distinction between life and death. "Memory," writes Nora, "is always a phenomenon of the present, a bond tying us to the eternal present; history is a representation of the past" (3). In an eternal present, there is no room for loss—which is what the Europeans expropriate, above all, from the Élékéiks. In a peculiarly modern paradox, the moderns mourn the immortality of the ancients they have immortalized. Modernity thus projects its primitives as the living image of its own death instinct, its desire for inertia (or the loss of loss). Typically, what colonizers discover is validation of their conception of history and their own place in it. Colonialism's "discovery" of a synchronic other has made possible—and has become inseparable from—modernity's "discovery" of a diachronic other. Both discoveries entail the sacrifice of difference among individual members of the groups whose identities are forged in the process: "the primitive," "the modern," "the savage," "the civilized." The distillation of this sacrifice into anecdote is the function of the colonial unconscious, the product of interwar France's imperial dream-work.

Cannibals in Babylon

René Crevel's Allegories of Exclusion

> In Babylon, according to Otto Rank, the most ancient temple was called the temple of the intestines, and it had the strength of a digestive tract. It is as if, from earliest antiquity, such a temple had been built to harbor the Surrealist object, for the most recent works by Dali on cannibalism have taught us that this object was made to be eaten.
>
> Crevel, *L'Esprit contre la raison*

In the work of Raymond Roussel's young contemporary, René Crevel, the exotic plays a role that is at once anecdotal and indicative of the mechanisms of repression and displacement that characterize the colonial unconscious. Like Roussel, Crevel reveals the process underlying the construction of the primitive in modern French culture, without managing to distance himself entirely from the ideological positions he depicts.

To a large extent, Crevel's work reflects the contradictions of the artistic movement with which he maintained a complex relationship until his suicide at the age of thirty-four. In the first *Manifeste du surréalisme*, André Breton praised René Crevel as one of those who had "fait acte de SUR- REALISME ABSOLU" (1985, 36); in the second *Manifeste*, he invoked the "valeur subversive" of Crevel's work (119) (a compliment perhaps not unrelated to the fact that Crevel was a cosignatory of the second manifesto). And this in spite of Breton's aversion to homosexuality and to novel writing, both activities in which Crevel engaged. An enthusiastic participant in Surrealist experiments with automatism, which were directly influenced by the psychoanalytic practice of free association, Crevel hailed Surrealist efforts to bring unconscious thought processes into waking life. In his essay "La période des sommeils" (Sleep experiments) Crevel explained that he was drawn to Surrealism "because, dialectic in its essence, Surrealism does not mean to sacrifice either dreams to action, or action to dreams, preferring instead to foster their synthesis" (1986, 276). But this synthetic vision, although an integral aspect of Surrealist thought, did not extend to the relationship between Surrealism and political practice. Try as he might, Crevel could not reconcile his artistic and political loyalties: unlike Aragon, he did not choose Communism to the exclusion of Surrealism; and, unlike Breton, he could not bring himself to reject Communism on artistic grounds. It may have been this irreconcilable difference that drove him to suicide in 1935, during the First International Congress of Writers for the Defense of Culture (Shattuck 1986, 21).

Nor did Surrealism's own dialectical view of the world extend to colonialism: on this question, the movement remained ambivalent and did not transcend the division between Western and non-Western cultures imposed by its exoticist aesthetic. On the one hand, the Surrealists joined forces to author collective tracts condemning colonial atrocities, and they protested against colonialism at happenings such as a 1925 banquet attended by Michel Leiris that erupted into a protest against the Rif War, and the "exposition anticoloniale," which, as we have seen, was planned to coincide with the 1931 Exposition coloniale. But at the same time, there was an undercurrent of primitivism running through Surrealist thought, a sensibility that implicitly devalued colonized cultures while ostensibly celebrating their difference (see Clifford 1988).

Crevel's work reflects, to some extent, Surrealism's ambivalence. Crevel's essays and political writings condemn the racism fostered by French colonialism and include the collaboratively written Surrealist tracts ("Ne Visitez pas l'Exposition coloniale" and "Premier bilan de l'Exposition coloniale") protesting the 1931 colonial exhibition (*Tracts surréalistes* 1980). Yet Crevel's work is not immune from the lure of exoticism: although it often appears to dismantle many of the presuppositions of primitivism (such as, notably, the opposition between the civilized and the savage), it also lapses at moments into what can only be interpreted as a celebration of the noble savage myth. In 1925, Crevel wrote in a review of a stage show:

> Grock, the Fratellinis—I am too aware of their artistry and talent, when what I am interested in is what lies behind it. I don't fault their tricks for being too well structured, but I wish I were not so aware of their structure. . . .
>
> As for my negroes, they do not work; instead, they joke around, expressing fear and affection by turns, and they delight in their brightly colored costumes. Thanks to them, we have been transported to another continent. (Crevel 1925, 65)

In interpreting the Africans' performance as natural and spontaneous, in stripping it, in other words, of its performative dimension, Crevel anticipates the discourse of voyeurism that would, as we have seen, pervade much of the commentary surrounding the colonial exhibitions of the 1930s. Similarly, a poem Crevel published in the review *Cap* in 1924 reveals a resistance to assimilation based on a romanticized image of cultural difference:

Métro
The negroes of my youth
stained the skies of France
while their mahogany flutes
played a sweet little tune.
But now the negroes have lost
even their pride in their color.
Yet, dressed in navy blue,
they still believe in happiness.
These children of warm countries
have today become
station masters of the metro.

In associating cultural differentiation with the whimsy of childhood, the poem evokes a wistful longing for a time when, presumably, African innocence was untainted by the corrupting force of civilization (as, perhaps, childhood was untainted by the harsh compromises of the adult world).

Nevertheless, exoticist moments such as these did not prevent Crevel from launching acerbic attacks on the exploitation inherent in the jazz-age cult of what James Clifford has called "Negrophilia" (Clifford 1994, 901–8): "Blacks are for whites the means to an end, sources of entertainment, like late-empire Roman slaves for their rich masters" (Crevel 1966, 96). Crevel's blind spots—his colonial unconscious—testify to the pervasive force of exoticist stereotypes, but they do not prevent him from developing an extensive critique, throughout his writings, of the exclusionary practices inherent in the construction of these stereotypes.

Literary history has shown that Crevel's own enduringly marginal status in the canon ironically enacts the exclusion thematized in his work. Crevel remains relatively obscure in France and is still virtually unknown in Great Britain and the United States; he is only briefly mentioned, if at all, in most studies of twentieth-century French literature.[1] When Crevel's work is taken into consideration, it is criticized for its lack of internal homogeneity. J. H. Matthews, writing of the 1927 novel *Babylone*, to which I now turn, insists that the work is "marred by intrusions which repeatedly disturb the narrative" (1966, 64); he laments, moreover, its "unevenness in tone and inconsistency of approach, [which] finally mar a work otherwise possessed of considerable potential" (66). The word "intrusions" presupposes the existence of an otherwise homogeneous text, whose self-containment is predicated on the distinction between inside and outside. But it is precisely this distinction, and its political repercussions, that *Babylone* calls into question.

The Tower of *Babylon*

In the autobiographical blurb inserted in the first edition of *Babylone*, Crevel wrote, "For future novels, René Crevel hopes to find characters as naked and vivid as the knives and forks that played the roles of men and women in his childhood games of make-believe" (cited in Chénieux-Gendron 1983, 229). By uniting nudity and silverware, two topoi commonly assigned to opposite ends of the spectrum used to determine how "civilized" a culture is, Crevel manages to undermine the implicitly hierarchical assumptions on which the notion of civilization is based.[2] In the novel that the blurb supplements, Crevel lays bare the association between, on the one hand, nudity and nature, and, on the other, clothing and civilization, by showing the extent to which the concept of nudity is a cultural construct. Similarly, the civilized refinement that silverware represents is undermined in *Babylone*'s scenes of bourgeois society, in which eating is depicted as an expression of otherwise repressed sexual desire. The novel's culinary metaphors culminate in images of cannibalism, a practice that literally blurs the boundary between individuals (and between dinner and diner), even as it is invoked as an absolute criterion to distinguish between groups. As with incest, a theme that floats just below the novel's surface, this failure to erect boundaries results in an absolute boundary between the "civilized" and the "savage": "they" are uncivilized because they eat other people, and "we" are civilized because we know that eating people is off limits. This distinction underwrites the exclusion of those deemed uncivilized from civilized—that is to say, the dominant—culture. *Babylone* depicts the twofold process of exclusion, which entails the imposition of unity on a given group, or the denial of difference among its members, and, at the same time, the imposition of differences between groups.

Babylone is an absurdist narrative recounted from the perspective of a little girl (referred to only as "la petite fille" and "l'enfant") whose father runs off with Cynthia, an unconventional English cousin, to the dismay of the child's staid bourgeois family. The household is further shaken up when the family summer home is broken into and when the child's grandmother, who begins the novel as a prim society woman and devoted wife to her authoritarian psychiatrist husband, elopes to Marseille with the young detective called in to investigate the robbery. Meanwhile, the child's abandoned mother, a meek, obedient woman, is paired up, for the sake of propriety, with a homely Protestant missionary based in Africa. The missionary sends a young Senegalese woman to live with what is left of the family, in the hope of winning her over to French spiritual values, but the missionary's moralistic plans are foiled when the young woman runs away and becomes a prostitute. The plot of this satire of bourgeois morality and the nuclear family, however, with its wild reversals and comical peripeteias, is almost an incidental aspect of the narrative, which is largely composed of the little girl's phantasmagorical daydreams.

The signifier "Babylon," like the biblical name to which it refers, has a variety of connotations in the novel. In the first place, it is used by the family's patriarchal grandfather to describe the household in which his wife has run off with a younger man, his niece by marriage has run off with his son-in-law, and the chambermaid has murdered the gardener after robbing the family: "The most respectable homes are metamorphosed into Babylon and the least prophylactic rendered impossible. Under my roof, under my very nose and beard, opium has been smoked, kerosene been drunk, and a hitherto upright magistrate has been debauched" (Crevel 1996, 90). In this context, the word "Babylon" serves as a condemnation of actions that have no place in the grandfather's rigidly constructed moral universe (the kerosene drinker evoking the *pétroleuses* of the Paris Commune, a political event that posed a threat to bourgeois values). The debauchery that has torn apart the "hitherto upright magistrate" [*magistrat jusqu'alors intègre*]—the adjective "intègre," in keeping with the biblical motif, suggesting a lost wholeness or plenitude—also tears apart the bourgeois family, disrupting the order that had once reigned supreme. The grandfather's words express his personal loss in terms of a loss of order and integrity: he projects his loss not only onto the household but also onto the magistrate with whom his wife has run off and who has gained what he himself has lost.

"Babylon" is also synonymous with utopia in the novel. It is what the grandmother christens the dream house that she and her lover plan to build in Marseille: "So we must have *terrasses*, terraces on which to stroll, to bathe ourselves completely in life and dreams. Terraces and even—why not?—hanging gardens all around the house, and this would be a property that we would call Babylon" (138–39). Here the hanging gardens evoke the luxury and opulence of the biblical city. For the newly emancipated grandmother, the word signifies the liberty to love how and whom she pleases. But it also harbors within it the fate of the biblical Babylon, which was destroyed by God's wrath. By the end of the novel, the word has become an incantation, sounding the grandmother's desperate recognition of the fact that truly utopian desire has no place in her meticulously ordered universe: "Babylon, Babylon, Babylon, Amie howls aloud her passion. She is placed in a straitjacket. Babylon. Babylon. Babylon" (154).

Above all, Babylon is Babel: the two words share an etymology (gate of God) and a geobiblical origin (Babylon is the city in which the Tower of Babel was built). In the Old Testament story (Gen. 11), the Semites attempt to build a tower high enough to reach God, who punishes this act of hubris by destroying the tower and condemning its builders to mutual incomprehensibility and confusion. Commonly understood to depict the introduction of division into an originally undivided world, this story has been interpreted quite differently by Jacques Derrida in his essay "Des Tours de Babel." Derrida's reading suggests that it is unity, not difference, which must be imposed from without, and that God's punishment merely restores division rather than inaugurates it. The Semites' claim to unity, according to Derrida, entails the eradication of difference: "By seeking to 'make a name for themselves,' to found both a universal language and a unique genealogy, the Semites hoped to bring reason to the world, and this reason can signify both a colonial violence (because they would universalize their idiom thus) and a pacific transparence of the human community' (Derrida 1985, 215).

By pointing out that the builders of the tower must "found" [*fonder*] a universal language," Derrida indicates the paradox at work in the Genesis story. To found something is to ground it in the specificity of a time and place, thus foreclosing the possibility of universality (both temporal and spatial). To say that a "universal language" must be imposed by a particular group is to expose the illusion that unity is a natural or universal phenomenon: "Before the deconstruction of Babel, the great Semitic family was in the process of building its empire, which it wanted to be universal, and its language, which it tried to impose on the universe as well" (Derrida 1985, 210). Derrida's assertion that unity must be founded (rather than found), in other words, that it is historically or culturally produced, undermines the association between, on the one hand, unity and nature, and, on the other, diversity and culture, suggesting that diversity is anterior to unity, and not the other way around.

Derrida's use of the colonial metaphor to characterize the imposition of unity, the generalization of a specificity (in his words, the "universalis[ation]" of an "idiome"), itself assigns to the word "colonial" a more generalized meaning that includes not only the historical and political act of colonialism but also all other eradications of difference both discursive and practical. The violence to which Derrida refers lies not, as might be expected, in the imposition of division into an otherwise homogeneous community but rather in the suppression of difference implicit in the construction of group identities.

The danger inherent in the imposition of unity on difference can be seen in another text which invokes the Babelian metaphor and which, although written in 1853, achieved the height of its popularity around the time Crevel wrote *Babylone*.[3] In his *Essai sur l'inégalité des races humaines*, which blames miscegenation for the deterioration of the white "race," Joseph-Arthur de Gobineau laments:

Even if we admit that it is better to turn a myriad of degraded beings into mediocre men than to preserve the race of princes whose blood is adulterated and impoverished by being made to suffer this dishonourable change, yet there is still the unfortunate fact that the change does not stop here; or when the mediocre men are once created at the expense of the greater, they combine with other mediocrities, and from such unions, which grow ever more and more degraded, is born a confusion which, like that of Babel, ends in utter impotence, and leads societies down to the abyss of nothingness. (Gobineau 1970, 140)

For Gobineau, this Babelian confusion is the result of a decline—not unlike the Judeo-Christian Fall—from an original, harmonious unity: the white race. History, he says, has taught that "all civilizations derive from the white race, that none can exist without its help, and that a society is great and brilliant only so far as it preserves the blood of the noble group that created it, provided that this group itself belongs to the most illustrious branch of our species" (140–41). Gobineau's theory of decay grounds itself in the tyranny of a lost plenitude, which privileges a particular sector of the human race as the unit of measure, or currency, for all others. In elevating the particular to the status of the universal, like the builders of the Tower of Babel according to Derrida, Gobineau's myth thus does what Roland Barthes accused modern bourgeois myths of doing. Barthes writes that "the very principle of myth [is that] it transforms history into nature" (1987, 129). He characterizes the function of myth itself as a form of colonialism, in which a polyvalent signifier is weighted with a single sense whose specificity is masked in the name of a general application: "One could say that language offers to myth an open-work meaning. Myth can easily insinuate itself into it and swell there: it is a robbery by colonization" (132).

When difference is cast in a negative relation to unity, when it is conceived as impurity, it becomes a criterion of exclusion. In Crevel's novel, this conception of difference is shown to underlie the opposition between "civilized" and "primitive" societies, an opposition whose main function is to legitimate the exclusionary practices of a dominant culture.

THE EMPIRE'S NEW CLOTHES

One of the bourgeois values most ridiculed in *Babylone* is that of physical modesty. Nudity, or near-nudity, is one of the features that makes Cynthia so attractive to the little girl and so despicable to her family. During a family meal, the grandmother scoffs: "Her dress, have you noticed Cynthia's dress? You'd think she was decked out for the Martinique sun instead of for the fogs of England, the last country of Europe, however, my dear brother-in-law used to say (the unfortunate father of this creature), where a certain notion of dignity is preserved. At any rate, our young slut won't die of the heat, with her three rags around her hips" (12).

Cynthia's style of dress is associated, in the eyes of the disapproving family, with the Caribbean, "the Martinique sun." The narrative ridicules the family's intolerance; it does not, however, question the association, implicit in the passage cited above, between nudity and the notion of the "primitive." This association appears again at the end of the novel, when the "rue de la négresse" (where the African woman who has been taken under the minister's wing practices prostitution) inspires the narrator's rhapsodic invocation of Marseille as a utopian Babylon in which nudity and sexual license are given free reign:

> One must leave, go on with one's life, and with each step taken in the sun, better and better learn to know that there is no sweeter oasis than the street of the Negress.
>
> In comparison with the sky, all is dust, and yet those booths of caresses were carpeted with a velvet humidity that remained eternally fresh. O day without a soul, there is only one road, that of the flesh, a road one travels thinking only of bodies against bodies, of rafts of nakedness there for other nakednesses.
>
> Babylon, Babylon, Babylon (153–54)

It is no accident that it is an African woman who provides the pretext for this homage to nudity. In an article titled "L'Afrique de René Crevel," Michel Carassou writes, "Crevel wishes to locate primitive nudity, which appears insolent only to those who confuse clothing with civilization" (1985, 12). The narrator of *Babylone*, embracing the traditional stereotype of the noble savage, a purely instinctual creature uncorrupted by social inhibitions, revels in the image of a sensuous Africa, seen through the nostalgic eyes of the Senegalese adolescent: "Her white eyes scorned the resinous pine of the linen room and returned in longing to a country planted with muscular thighs, with carnal trees, whose leaves are hands, tough and skillful in their caresses" (103). Crevel's Africa is a world in which the human body is part of the earth, where thighs and the hands that caress them belong to the same organism. These "carnal trees" know no inhibitions, no restrictions—in other words, no repression mechanism, which suggests that the African libido (for such a monolithic entity in fact seems to be presupposed in *Babylone*) has much more of a free reign than its French counterpart. Yet, five years after the publication of *Babylone*, Crevel attacked this very stereotype. In a 1932 essay, "De la volupté coloniale au patriotisme de l'inconscient" (From colonial pleasure to the patriotism of the unconscious), he ridiculed the notion advanced in a 1931 psychiatric journal that the African psyche is less complex than the European one, that Africans are completely instinctual creatures devoid of an unconscious (Crevel 1986, 137–47).

The apparent inconsistency between Crevel's critique of primitivism in his essay and the seeming celebration of primitivism in the novel is actually resolved in another passage of *Babylone*, which can be read against Crevel's own use of stereotype. While fantasizing about the lives being led by those who have abandoned her (her father and Cynthia, her mother and the missionary), the little girl sees a painting of a young African man, an image that will reappear later in a dream scene as an allegorical figure named Avenir (Future). Mesmerized by the portrait, the little girl

> fell in love. At first she did not know with whom, but soon she came to know it was with a colored boy. She loved him. She had seen his portrait. He was called "Le Nègre." The eighteenth century had already foreseen him. La Tour had painted his face, his bust. He had clothed him. But under the muslin of his shirt, the rose velvet of his coat, it was easy to guess into what shoulders the neck curved. The head was in three-quarter view. A topaz elongated the one visible ear. The eyes were sad because of this exile in a frame, in the very heart of a drab town. (101–2)

This passage, which refers to a pastel by Maurice Quentin de la Tour titled *Portrait d'un Nègre*, suggests that the young man's nudity represents a kind of authentic self that can only be intimated beneath the layers of European clothes. It is this imaginary image, the image beneath the image, that the little girl loves. Yet both images, that of a slave clad in European garb and that of the nude African beneath the clothes, are "exile[d] in a frame," caught within the boundaries of representation. Crevel may be proposing a "natural" African self in opposition to an artificial European overlay—references to the chiffon and pink velvet, suggestive of the highly ornate rococo style, reinforce the impression of artificiality—but the very image he uses, that of nudity, to represent this authenticity is itself highly codified, an exoticist commonplace. In this sense, then, and paradoxically, the noble savage's nudity serves the same function as the layers of European clothing in the painting: the two images, seen or imagined, are equally romanticized, equally artificial.

IMPERIAL BANQUETS

Babylone announces its preoccupation with things culinary in the title of its first chapter, "Monsieur Couteau, Mademoiselle Fourchette." The title refers to a game of make-believe played by the little girl, whose musings, true to Crevel's authorial blurb, are peopled with cutlery:

> The knife is Papa. The white part that cuts is his shirt; the black part you hold in your hand is his trousers. If the white part that cuts was the same as the black part, I could say he was in pajamas, but it's too bad there's no way to do that.
>
> The fork is Cynthia. . . . The part you stick into the things you want to take off your plate, that's Cynthia's hair. She has a pretty bosom that moves up and down because she is out of breath. Papa is very happy. He caresses Cynthia, and he laughs, because he thinks it is two little birds she has closed up in her dress. (7)

Claude Lévi-Strauss has described the function of cutlery as that of insulating the user from an outside world coded as impure. After a lengthy study of culinary habits among Amerindian cultures in *The Origin of Table Manners*, he concludes that table utensils protect the user from contamination "between the social person and his or her own body, in which nature is unleashed" (Lévi-Strauss 1979a, 505). The images that fill the little girl's daydream can thus be seen as a metaphor for the dream itself, which protects the child from the world around her by constructing a private universe that does not admit loss.

Culinary metaphors are used throughout the novel to establish self-contained groups that affirm their "purity" by maintaining boundaries between inside and outside. The little girl's family, for example, is introduced on the first page of the novel as "a family that drank only water, suspected the effects of pepper, banished Worcestershire sauce from the table, as well as pickles and even mustard, but willingly held forth between fruit and cheese upon the question of social hygiene" (3). Characters are often identified with what they consume, by means of epithets that indicate their social and moral status. The chambermaid accused of stealing the grandmother's prized heirloom bracelet is referred to as "la buveuse de pétrole" (the kerosene drinker); likewise, the episode in which the Senegalese girl manages to escape from the moralistic clutches of her benefactors concludes, "Thus did the daughter of forthright cannibals outwit the cunning of the drinkers of water" (36). As this quotation demonstrates, the cannibalistic epithet is used to create a stark contrast between the child's family and those who pose a moral threat to its value system, which is clearly class-based. Cannibalism is associated with the transgressive danger Cynthia represents: like her clothing, which evokes "the Martinique sun," Cynthia's eating habits link her to the "forthright cannibals" whose appetites threaten the moral integrity of the little girl's family.

In another passage, cannibalistic consumption is associated with a transgression of the boundaries of class when Cynthia's mother appears in a dream in the form of a talking fish, lamenting her daughter's behavior: "Cynthia, my daughter, . . . at this very moment is admitting to herself that she is no better than a crane [*une grue*]. A crane. Cranes, she believes, live on fish. Here you can see the danger of the metaphor of words" (59–60). This "danger" manifests itself just moments later, as the metaphorical meaning of the word "grue"—prostitute—gives way to its literal origin as a piscivorous crane: "Oh, heavens, I am dying. She is eating me. Sh-she is-s-s eat-eat-eating m-me. Sh-shh-sh-sh-she i-i-i-i-s ea-t-t-i-n-g-g-g-g m-m-m-m-me" (60). Although this most transgressive form of consumption, cannibalism, is couched in the nonthreatening form of one animal preying on another, the horror of the act is heightened by the fact that it involves a child consuming her mother: in fact, the fish's drawn-out cry (in the French, "man-man-an-an-an-an-g-g-g-g-g-g-g-g-g-ge") recalls its maternal relationship—"ma(n)man"—to its devourer. The transgressive nature of the act is further reinforced by its juxtaposition with another example of the "danger" of metaphors: "Thus was our great-aunt Laura made a demimondaine through the fault of a predestined name in a time when women who misbehaved were called 'lorettes' " (60). The two pairs of signs established through a formal resemblance between signifiers (grue / grue; Laura / lorette) are linked to one another by a common element, that of promiscuity: grue (promiscuous woman) / grue (crane), and Laura / lorette (promiscuous woman). Named for the cathedral Notre Dame de Lorette, in whose vicinity once lived a number of demimondaines, the term "lorette" conveys sexual and working-class connotations.

Sexualized eating in the novel often poses a direct threat to class-based hierarchies. In one of the little girl's daydreams, inspired by a children's story, the narrator intervenes: "Their Majesties who open a ball must cut their wrists, or their lips, rather than yield to any one of those temptations so natural to the common herd [*ceux du vulgaire*] that the little girl was not in the least surprised the first time she saw the gardener savagely biting the chambermaid's neck" (35). In this way, the working class is set up in the novel as an attractive-repulsive, exoticized "other" whose position vis-à-vis the bourgeoisie is analogous, and whose behavior is similar, to that of a cannibal.

The grandmother's sexual transgression is not in itself enough to ostracize her from polite society; it is only when her sexuality takes the form of attempted cannibalism that she is finally excluded from the ruling class: she is pronounced "folle" after running up to a priest in the middle of a church service and sinking her teeth into his neck, yelling, "White meat, beautiful white meat!" (146). Not uncoincidentally, the first signs of the grandmother's sexual reawakening—which culminates in her elopement with a younger man named, significantly, Petitdemange—can be glimpsed in a description of her eating habits. Two paragraphs after the fish dream episode, the grandmother repeats the devoration scene, assuming the role of the ravenous English woman: "Meanwhile, a bite of toast. An arrogant tooth attacked it. The tooth of a lion" (60–61). The resemblance suggested between the women in their roles as ravenous consumers foreshadows the grandmother's total identification with her former nemesis, in which she imitates the younger woman's hairstyle, gestures, and speech patterns (71–73).

Eating seems to be at the center not only of the grandmother's transformation but of a whole host of "unexpected metamorphos[e]s" (73) in which unstable identities become indistinguishable from their structural opposites. The object of one such transformation is the family cook, who is found lying bound and gagged after the theft of an heirloom bracelet containing a lock of the empress Eugénie's hair. The narrative interposes a description of the cook with speculation about the death of Eugénie and Napoleon's son, the prince Napoleon, purported to have died in southern Africa. The imbrication of the two scenarios creates a composite image of the corpulent cook-as-imperial-explorer:

The Zulus had killed Eugénie's son. . . . With their arrows they assassinate explorers, then sit in a circle around a big fire and sing "Zulu, zulu, zulu," while the prisoners slowly cook. The Zulus are cannibals, but if the grandmother, who couldn't distinguish the blood of a chicken from that of a cook (whom she had, moreover, compared to a shoulder of mutton), had been served a thumb, being told it was the drumstick of some fowl, or been given a piece of the arm in the guise of filet of a veal, would she not have eaten this flesh? (36)

One of the most striking things about this passage is the confusion it cultivates between carnivorousness and cannibalism. It is significant that the locus of such confusion is the cook—agent, in anthropological terms, of the transition to culture, or what sets humans apart from other animals. The grandmother's inability to distinguish between her servant and various meat dishes bestializes the woman's body, ironically negating the "civilizing" function the cook represents by virtue of her ability to transform (nonhuman) animals into cultural objects, a transformation that produces a concomitant transformation of human animals into cultural beings.

The cook's bestialization is only one of several reversals performed in the passage. The references to the roasting imperial prince and the bleeding cook combine to produce an image of the cook crackling on a spit: as the cook herself is cooked, a cultural agent becomes a cultural object. This reversal is performed by the juxtaposition of the onomatopoeic signifier for the sound of the cook's gushing blood, "glouglou," with the chanting of the name "Zoulou," a juxtaposition reinforced by the rhyming phonemes "ou-ou": " 'Zulu, zulu, zulu, zulu . . . ' The servant was so fat, so flushed, that had the bandits disemboweled her, the blood would have flowed from her wound, as from an actual spigot, for at least a good quarter of an hour. 'Zulu, zulu, zulu, zulu, gurgle-gur-gur [*Zoulou, zoulou, zoulou, glouglou-glou-glou*]' " (36). Like the association of the signs "Laura" and "lorette" in the grandmother's dream, the formal resemblance between the signifiers "glouglou" and "Zoulou" suggests that the signifieds are interchangeable. On the surface, the equation of the name Zoulou with the sound of spurting blood suggests that it is the prince Napoleon's blood that is being spilled. But the profusion of reversals in the passage necessarily affects this image as well, opening it up to the interpretive possibility of inversion—which would yield the (more historically logical) image of Napoleon spilling the blood of his Zulu captors.

A similar ambiguity is evoked in a passage that follows shortly after, and refers back to, the scene in which the grandmother discovers the cook bleeding on the floor. This time it is the grandmother herself who has undergone a transformation, as if infected by the metaphorical reversals taking place in the text: "She had forgotten her initial terror on the kitchen threshold at the sight of the garroted body, which the promise of an empire could not have persuaded her to touch. She was able to affirm, and in all sincerity, that on the battlefield of the tiles she had felt as much at her ease and as majestic [*tout aussi impériale*] as Napoleon at Austerlitz. The stains . . . had made her wonder if they were the blood of chicken or servant" (40). In this passage, the grandmother is compared explicitly with Napoleon, an equation reinforced by the words "empire" and "impériale." The subsequent reference back to the woman's confusion between her cook and a chicken she herself might eat suggests that the imperial function is inseparable from that of consumer, thus reinforcing the earlier reversal made possible by the Zoulou-glouglou juxtaposition, in which it is the imperial prince who consumes the cannibals. Similarly, when the missionary Mac-Louf is proselytizing in Africa, the African villagers are shown baring "their fine cannibalistic teeth" (99)—when just a few sentences earlier, the same people are likened to "chickens [that] collect behind servant-girls in the hope of being fed" (99). Of course, the chickens that hope to be fed are destined to become food themselves, just as, by extension, the "cannibal-toothed" Africans will in the end be swallowed up by the colonial system and its network of ecclesiastic representatives.

CANNIBALISM AND ITS DISCONTENTS

Crevel's evocations of cannibalism as a metaphor for negotiations of identity and difference were no doubt influenced by similar imagery used in psychoanalysis, with which he was familiar in both theory and practice.[4] Notably, the taboos of cannibalism and incest are yoked together in Freud's highly speculative account of the origins of civilization. In his essay "The Return of Totemism in Childhood" in *Totem and Taboo*, cannibalism is demetaphorized, like the crane that eats the grandmother's sister in *Babylone*.[5] The infamous passage in which Freud traces the incest prohibition to an originary parricide committed by a band of jealous brothers concludes, "Cannibal savages as they were, it goes without saying that they devoured their victim as well as killing him" (Freud

1950, 142). It is this act of cannibalism that enables the brothers to identify with their father and internalize his restriction of the women in the group, leading to the institutionalization of exogamy:

> The violent primal father had doubtless been the feared and envied model of each one of the company of brothers: and in the act of devouring him they accomplished their identification with him, and each one of them acquired a portion of his strength. The totem meal, which is perhaps mankind's earliest festival, would thus be a repetition and a commemoration of this memorable and criminal deed, which was the beginning of so many things—of social organization, of moral restrictions and of religion. (142)

Such a great deal rides on this uncharacteristically sweeping affirmation that Freud feels compelled to defend it in a footnote: "This hypothesis, which has such a monstrous air, of the tyrannical father being overwhelmed and killed by a combination of his exiled sons was also arrived at by Atkinson (1903, 220f.) as a direct implication of the state of affairs in Darwin's primal horde" (142n). Yet Freud cites other scholars in defense of only the parricide in his theory, *not the cannibalism*, which, as he says, "goes without saying." The literal ingestion of the father is taken for granted, and indeed it is as crucial for Freud's theory of a phylogenetic unconscious as the infant's attempt to ingest its mother's breast is for the development of an individual, or ontogenetic, unconscious in Melanie Klein's concept of the "cannibalistic stage," in which "the fear of being devoured by the father derives from the projection of the infant's impulses to devour his objects. In this way first the mother's breast (and the mother) becomes in the infant's mind a devouring object" (Klein 1948, 117).

Unlike the Oedipus complex, which Freud claims is as timeless as it is universal, and unlike his (revised) assertion that most accounts of childhood sexual abuse have no basis in reality (1966, 370), Freud's etiology of the incest taboo is grounded in a supposedly real event. This event, internalized and eternalized in the form of collective guilt, is credited with engendering the double-pronged Oedipal prohibition:

> A sense of guilt made its appearance, which in this instance coincided with the remorse felt by the whole group. The dead father became stronger than the living one had been. . . . What had up to then been prevented by his actual existence was thenceforward prohibited by the sons themselves, in accordance with the psychological procedure so familiar to

us in psycho-analysis under the name of 'deferred obedience'. They revoked their deed by forbidding the killing of the totem, the substitute for their father; and they renounced its fruits by resigning their claim to the women who had now been set free. (Freud 1950, 143)

It is only through an act of bona fide cannibalism—an act so obviously essential to Freud's theory that it can go (almost) without saying—that the incest prohibition can develop.

Perhaps Freud's associative leap was motivated by the fact that, like incest, cannibalism does not respect boundaries. Marc Augé, citing Lévi-Strauss's observation that in many cultures the acts of eating and copulation are associated, notes that the logical extension of this analogy is the association between cannibalism and incest (Augé 1972, 140). Both cannibalism and incest (which first appears in Crevel's novel as the union between the little girl's father and "la cousine Cynthia," who is either the father's cousin or the little girl's cousin and thus the father's niece) are based on a problematic resemblance (between diner and dinner, or sexual partners who are related to one another) that results in differentiation, or ostracization from the "civilized" world.

BICOLORE

Incest resurfaces in *Babylone*, not surprisingly, in a dream the little girl has while traveling with the young Senegalese servant to meet the three couples returning from honeymoon voyages: the child's grandmother and lover Petitdemange, the mother and her missionary husband Mac-Louf, and the father and Cynthia. In this dream, La Tour's "nègre" appears nude on the train, having thrown his rococo clothes out the window. The figure, who in this passage is called Avenir (Future), is accompanied by his allegorical counterpart, an oneiric vision of the Senegalese woman, who does not appreciate his amorous attention to another passenger: "Already his hand lightly touched the nape of a neck. But his older sister, Negro as well, named Memory, became jealous (for, according to Mac-Louf, incest was an everyday occurrence in Africa) and with her traitorous hands she squeezed a mauve and maroon throat" (109). Future's affectionate gesture, the stroke of a neck, doubles back on itself in a deadly mirror image when he is strangled. The African woman, who has failed to assimilate into a French bourgeois milieu, cuts a threatening figure as Memory—specifically, as the memory of France's colonial past coming back to haunt it, victim transformed into victimizer.

Like hysterical symptoms of repression, memory in Crevel's novel is literally inscribed on the body. After murdering Avenir, Mémoire is raped in a cemetery by a workman she meets, and then discovers that the encounter has "stamped the corpses' names in letters of dust on her nudity" (110). Crevel's allegory represents memory as the inscription of loss—the names of the dead—on the body, an inscription that renders the intelligible sensible. This scene of corporeal inscription recalls that both the Senegalese servant's "difference" from her employers, which prevents her from assimilating into their bourgeois milieu, and her "resemblance" with other Africans are made possible by the encoding of her body as a sign, and the concomitant construction of "race" as an aesthetic category.

This corporeal semiotics is, as we have seen, a central feature of the colonial aesthetic. Whereas semiotics has shown that difference is necessary to create meaning, history has shown that it is the sacrifice of differentiation among individuals, and its displacement onto groups, that makes the classification of human beings possible. In a 1930 essay, "Bobards et fariboles" (Stuff and nonsense), Crevel mocks the prevailing tendency during the interwar period to classify human beings into biological categories: "We are all familiar with the face of France. We know the exact color of her hair, even though it is hidden beneath a phrygian bonnet. We know that Lady France is darker than Germany (despite the dark Berlin Jewish women) and lighter than Italy (in spite of the northern blondes and the Venetian redheads)" (1986, 110). Crevel's caricature of racial stereotyping has implications that extend beyond his critique of nationalism. He concludes, "Any classification of human beings, especially the kind based on the prism of skin colors, has, to this day, never been anything but a pretext for the most sinister abuses" (1986, 110–11). In Crevel's Marseille / Babylone, the Reverend Mac-Louf insists, "Don't get me wrong, I have nothing against having creatures of all skin colors here" (151).

Crevel had been grappling with the role of the aestheticized body in race-thinking at least since 1922, when an image presented itself to him in the form of a "pensée parlée," the spoken equivalent of automatic writing (see Crevel 1986, 273–74). Crevel would recycle the image of the "négresse aux bas blancs [negress with white stockings]" several times, because it served as a forceful expression of the race-thinking and binary logic that subtend colonial discourse. A transcription of one of Crevel's "pensées parlées" appeared in the journal *Littérature* in 1922 with the heading "Samedi 7 octobre. *Parlé*."[6] The text begins, "The negress with white stockings loves paradoxes!" The paradox in question turns out to be a strictly binary one: "We have had, however, in our eyes, those stones and sand and this red festoon itself festooned, and, who knows, this Negress might have had a blue eye, which would have made a tricolored flag, but, for God's sake, no flag; the paradox is in two colors" (1974, 183). It is for more than its tricoloredness that Crevel opposes the French flag to the "négresse aux bas blancs." The latter is excluded from the privileges enjoyed by white French citizens because of the binary logic ("deux couleurs") that pits insiders against outsiders, "us" against "them." Here Crevel invokes the purely symbolic function of skin color, which is shown to be as arbitrary as any other sign yet invoked as sufficient justification for the discriminatory practices of the *métropole*.

These practices often resulted in objectification. In "De la volupté coloniale au patriotisme de l'inconscient," Crevel elaborates on the socioeconomic position of women of color in the *métropole*, describing their relegation to the status of commodities, part of bourgeois decor: "The negress, in the metropolitan brothels where she is confined by the almighty white man, is put in her place like her sister of bronze who bears electricity at the foot of the red-carpeted, gold-railed staircases, which are the perfect expression of self-satisfaction that characterized the turn of the twentieth century" (1966, 96). The woman of color is "à sa place" in the way Henri Fayol imagined workers in his Tayloresque vision of the factory and the world. By likening African women to commodities, Crevel underscores their exchange value in a binarized colonial culture that perceives them to be interchangeable—*indifférentes*.

THE POLITICS OF INDIFFERENCE

In his attack on national stereotyping, Crevel insisted that the potential for violence lay not in differentiation itself but in the systematization of difference, the classification "that assembles the features of a continent" (1986, 110) and that allows for differentiation only between groups, not within them. It is in such deadly indifference that *Babylone* draws to a close. As the little girl, now a woman, contemplates flinging herself into the Mediterranean, the novel's final sentence announces a rivalry between her and the city she has rejected: "A woman, a city, compete in indifference" (156). The woman and the city of Marseille, companions in neglect, are also opponents in similitude.[7] They are adversaries, but their differences are the same. The title of the novel's final chapter, "Le Triomphe indifférent," sums up the aporia that such a competition represents.

As the Christ-like "Femme-enfant,"dressed in burlap and wearing a crown of straw, stands at the water's edge picturing herself as Ophelia, the city of Marseille, like its biblical counterpart, is depicted in an analogous state of decay. This decay stems from "indifférence," an affect certainly, but also, literally, a lack of difference. But unlike the decline of differentiation among peoples that threatened Gobineau's superior white race, in Crevel, threatening "indifference" stems from the failure to distinguish among people within a group rather than the too-rigid barriers between groups. Crevel's Marseille is an agglomeration of mutually exclusive groups and isolated individuals: there are the over-the-hill prostitutes, "incredibly wretched souls, corseted in worldly indifference" (150); and there are the younger, practicing prostitutes, headed by the Senegalese woman (151–52). Then there is the Femme-enfant, whose misery makes her "indifferent in the blaze of summer, to the hot coals of thirst, to the smoke of hunger" (148). And finally, there is the young dock worker whom the Femme-enfant snubs, whose "indifférence" is expressed in terms of resemblance:

> A lad who resembled at the same time the one of Agrippa d'Aubigné Street and the father, with skin the color of his hair and eyes the color of Havana's sky, he alone had looked gently on her.
> He had the pride of those who load and unload ships, his muscles outlined under the coat of tan the sun had woven on his skin. (155)

Despite the dock worker's apparent sympathy, the young woman defensively keeps him at bay, grouping him with the three male figures who have rejected her: her father, the young man in La Tour's portrait, and the "young whistling workman" (104) who shares a social origin with the dock worker and who had rebuked the little girl's desire in favor of the Senegalese woman he would later rape (in the allegorical form of Mémoire) in the cemetery. Repeated use of variations of "indifférent" in these passages links the word's affective meaning, which resonates at the level of characterization and plot, to its literal meaning (lack of difference).

Like La Tour's "nègre," the dock worker is imagined nude by the little girl. This image of nudity beneath clothing appears as well in the description of the whistling workman, which invokes the La Tour portrait explicitly: "The child becoming a woman blushed, for she thought that under his canvas jacket, which did not permit a stitch of underwear to be seen, the man who dared to stare at her was perhaps nude. But we are always naked under something, she suddenly realized. The Negro in Geneva was nude under his old rose velvet" (104). The dock worker's nudity marks him, exposing his "hair-colored" skin, which here can only mean dark (a lyrical passage on page 112 begins, "Marseilles, brown of skin"). The young man's dark, bare skin links him to the "nègre" and the "jeune ouvrier siffleur." The man's dark nudity is a source of attraction to the young woman, but this attraction can only remind her of the other men she has desired and whom she has lost.

It is as protection against just this kind of loss that the little girl's daydreams function. Her vision of eating utensils (Mr. Knife, Miss Fork) conjures up surrogates of the people who have left her (her father, Cynthia), protecting her from the world around her by constructing a private, self-contained universe in which the losses that threaten to destroy her are denied. Lévi-Strauss, it will be recalled, described the function of cutlery as insulating the user from the outside world, suggesting, with more than a tinge of nostalgia, that it was not always this way: "If the origin of table manners, and more generally that of correct behaviour, is to be found, as I think I have shown, in deference towards the world . . . it follows that the inherent ethic of the myths runs counter to the ethic we profess today. . . . *For, since childhood, we have been accustomed to fear impurity as coming from without*" (1979a, 507; my emphasis). *Babylone* represents this fear of a threatening invasion in personal terms, at the level of characterization, with the young protagonist shrinking from contact with people she fears will cause her emotional distress. But the novel also paints a clear picture of the cultural implications of this mechanism, through the allegory of cannibalism.

In this sense, then, silverware, coded to represent civilized consumption, and its structural opposite, cannibalism, coded to represent uncivilized consumption, have a similar function: the construction and protection of a self-proclaimed interior from invasion from without.

In "Les Métamorphoses du vampire," Augé observes that cannibalism is a phenomenon that is always attributed to others but never to one's "own" culture (1972, 129). By showing the extent to which modern, bourgeois society is subject to its own cannibalistic impulses, Crevel succeeded in undermining cannibalism's status as what Augé calls "le fait des autres" (129). Like incest, cannibalism is pushed outside "civilized society" because it does not respect differences; it is the embodiment of colonial violences both literal and figurative, the embodiment of a culture turned on itself. To the extent, then, that it allegorizes the function of stereotype, which effaces difference within groups in order to establish differences between them, Crevel's cannibalistic imagery represents the ultimate colonial violence—a violence that has little to do with the consumption of human flesh.

CHAPTER 4

꿏㮰

A Colonial Princess

Josephine Baker's French Films

Mon prochain rôle? La Dame blanche!

Josephine Baker, *Pour Vous*

In 1988, François Mitterrand's reelection campaign produced a video clip depicting great moments in French history (of which Mitterrand's reelection, presumably, was to represent the culmination). There, among the rapid-fire barrage of photos depicting the usual assortment of barricades, resistance fighters, and puffy-sleeved novelists, appear at least four different images of Josephine Baker, preening for the camera, clad (if at all) in a tiny skirt made of banana skins. Icon of the jazz age, she seems to embody all that is exotic and daring, the heady exuberance of a brief moment in which France was no longer, nor quite yet again, at war. She is an instantly recognizable figure, a visual sound bite that sums up an era. But although her name can be found in the index of virtually any

Figure 5. *Josephine Baker dancing the Charleston at the Folies Bergère. Courtesy Bibliothèque du Film, Paris.*

book on French history or culture of the period, she is almost never mentioned except in passing, her impact rarely discussed seriously or analyzed in depth. Josephine Baker is usually considered part of the decor of interwar French culture but hardly ever the main attraction. Yet her influence on that culture was considerable, and her position within it can tell us a great deal about the formation of the colonial unconscious in twentieth-century France.

Baker's success in 1925 with the Revue nègre was followed by a triumphant run at the Folies Bergère in 1926–27; her popularity in the music hall was rivaled only by that of the legendary Mistinguett. In addition to *Zouzou* (1934) and *Princesse Tam-Tam* (1935), both popular successes and both written for her, she appeared in three short silent films: *La Folie du jour* (1926) and *La Revue des revues* (1927), both composed entirely of footage from her stage shows, and *La Sirène des tropiques* (1927), a feature film that costarred Pierre Batcheff. (Baker also had a cameo role in *Fausse alerte*, made in 1939.) One of the first media figures whose image was actively marketed, Baker was an industry unto herself. She inspired or endorsed products such as the Josephine Baker shoe, a hair gel called Bakerfix, and a cosmetics line designed to darken the skin; even bananas bore stickers announcing, "Josephine Baker is Zouzou" (see Haney 1981, 185 and 192; Stovall 1996). She inspired fashion designers, who created dresses such as the Zouzou and La Créole, after her title role in a 1935 play; she lent her name to a nightclub mentioned in many contemporary accounts as the place to see and be seen; and her signature song, "J'ai deux amours," was so well known that its lyrics were used in a print advertisement for thermoses. Her recipes for pancake syrup (spelled "Hote cake syroup") and corned beef hash ("Empty the contents of a can of corned beef hash . . . ") were even published in a celebrity recipe book, which appears to have placed more emphasis on the name recognition of its contributors than on their culinary skills (Derys 1929).

Baker was so popular, I want to suggest, precisely because she was so hard to place; a floating signifier of cultural difference, she represented many different things to different people. Alberto Capatti describes her polymorphous appeal thus: "She represents black beauty, Yankee freedom, and New Orleans blues; she's a jungle girl from the wilds of the Casino de Paris and, in her own special way, a cordon-bleu chef" (Capatti 1989, 206). Baker's enormous popularity owed much to her cosmopolitan identity: she could evoke Africa, the Caribbean, the United States, and France, by turns or all at once as the occasion required. Even within the limited scope of her two feature film roles, which are the subject of this chapter, Baker was associated with a variety of cultural personas, layered on top of one another: in *Zouzou*, she plays a Martinican who, as a music-hall performer, assumes the identity of a Haitian; and in *Princesse Tam-Tam*, she plays a Tunisian shepherdess who pretends to be a princess from the mythical land of Parador. Both films thematize cultural influence, equating assimilation with the adoption of an artificial identity, a performative persona that is not one's "own."

In the January 3, 1935, issue of *Pour Vous*, in the humor section, the following statement is attributed (probably falsely) to Baker: "Mon prochain rôle? La Dame blanche!": ("My next role? The White Woman!"). Interpreted using postidentitarian logic, this assertion would suggest that race is always a role to be played, a mask to be put on; but, conversely, in the logic of *Zouzou* and *Princesse Tam-Tam*, the statement could also imply that beneath the assumed racial identity lies a "real" racial makeup, an essential identity that produces an irreducible gap between the authentic and the assumed, perceptible to those who refuse to suspend their disbelief.

STAGING COMMUNITY IN *ZOUZOU*

Dismissed by contemporary critics as a conventional Hollywood knock-off, *Zouzou* was a popular success when it opened in 1934. The press screening of the Marc Allégret film was held on December 13, and the film opened the following week; on December 31, the owners of the theater at which it had an exclusive engagement could boast, "To date, 54,245 people have seen *Zouzou*, starring Josephine Baker" (*Comoedia*). Perhaps because of its popularity, however, the film has been practically ignored by film historians; one could say that its very visibility has prevented it from being examined closely. This paradox is reflected in—or, more accurately, on—the book *Générique des années 30*, whose ingenious cover, made up to look like the credits of a phantom film, displays the name "Zouzou," but both character and film are virtually absent within the book (Lagny, Rapars, and Sorlin 1986).

Similarly, the character Zouzou's colonial status is at once displayed and concealed in the diegetic performances that frame the film. In the opening sequence, set in a circus, a young, dark-skinned Zouzou and a little white boy (characters who, for the rest of the film, are portrayed as adults) are displayed in a freak show as "a miracle of nature," twins from Polynesia born of "a Chinese woman and a redskin [*peau-rouge*]." We soon learn that the children were actually adopted by the kind-hearted ringmaster, Papa Mélé, who responds to the children's inquiries about their origins by explaining that although they have different "pères," he alone is their "papa": "A father," he says, "is a papa you've

Figure 6. *Zouzou and Jean as children with Papa Mélé. Courtesy Bibliothèque du Film, Paris. All rights reserved.*

never met." This distinction between two modes of parenting allegorizes the colonial discourse of assimilation, equating the children's biological fathers with their countries of origin, whereas their adoptive father, their "papa," represents *la plus grande France*, clasping all its children in an egalitarian embrace. Conversely, the film's final scene points to assimilation gone awry, as a lovelorn, grown-up Zouzou, clad in a few strategically placed ostrich feathers and swinging from a perch in a giant birdcage, performs before an adoring music-hall audience her signature song, "Haïti," a mournful tribute to lost happiness. Unlike films in which the colonies serve as little more than a backdrop for the adventures of a French hero trying to escape a checkered past (*cinéma colonial*), *Zouzou* invites film viewers to sympathize with the joys and suffering of its eponymous heroine, who struggles to find a place in French society, which neither rejects her outright nor accepts her completely.

The rather predictable plotline follows Zouzou's meteoric rise to stardom when she is "discovered" while delivering laundry to a music hall, where her adoptive brother Jean (played by Jean Gabin) works as a lighting technician. The fact that she is originally from Martinique does not seem to hinder her success; in fact, apart from an allusion to her as "une belle Créole," race is never mentioned. Yet the film shows us what it will not tell us. Zouzou has the misfortune of falling in love with Jean, who, though full of brotherly affection for her, pairs up romantically with her best friend, a white woman. Although a sexual union between Zouzou and Jean appears to be precluded by their familial circumstances, it is racial difference that proves to be the ultimate obstacle. It has often been observed that colonial subjects, except for the occasional femme fatale, are virtually nonexistent in the *cinéma colonial* (see Lagny et al. 135–36). In *Zouzou*, the colonial comes home, in a sort of return of the repressed that prefigures postwar immigration (and repeats images that the French would remember from the colonial exhibition of 1931 and would see again at the 1937 World's Fair). But perhaps because they are staged, displayed in plain sight like Poe's purloined letter, the film's colonial dimension, and the questions of national identity it invokes, are all but hidden from view.

In 1934, the year *Zouzou* was released, traditional structures of community were being threatened by both the right and the left; between the right-wing leagues and the Popular Front, blueprints for new communities were projected onto the ruins of the Third Republic. Film was rapidly creating new representations of community as well as new communities of spectators. The transition from silent to sound film in the early 1930s, and the linguistic barriers that this transition brought to the fore, played into the debate over national identity, eliciting some hostile reactions that fed into a more general nostalgia for a community perceived to be on the wane. This nostalgia is at the heart of *Zouzou*.

Bread and Cinema

Entertainment forms are expressions of community, forums in which people interact in conscious affirmation of their shared experience. The different entertainment forms depicted in *Zouzou* represent different modes of community based on varying degrees of intimacy between performers and spectators, ranging from a formal distinction, in the case of the music hall, to a more porous division, in the case of the circus, to complete identification in participatory forms such as the *bal populaire*. Just as the music hall imposes a separation between spectacle and audience, it symbolizes a break with popular tradition, posing a threat to cultural continuity (for a certain class, that is, because the privileged classes in France have always had access to theatrical forms).

Dudley Andrew has described the mystique that the music hall cultivates, "tak[ing] its cue from the modern theatre, masking its performers behind curtains so as to present them dramatically or mysteriously. A hidden technology of lighting, décor and music assists the performers from a world beyond" (Andrew 1992, 24–25). In contrast to the music hall, Andrew observes, in the circus "everything remains in view" (24). In *Zouzou*, the circus is associated with innocence and openness, with days gone by—an association reinforced by its temporal coincidence with Zouzou and Jean's childhood. When Zouzou and Jean are adults, the circus can be invoked only nostalgically, in the context of loss. While working as a baby-sitter before her big break, Zouzou entertains her little charge by pretending to be a circus clown; when the child asks what has become of the circus in which she used to perform, Zouzou replies, "Bankruptcy." When she tells the child that the real clown on whom her imitation is based has died, we know she is speaking of her biological father, who was a clown in Mélé's circus. "Can clowns die, too?" the child asks. "Of course," Zouzou replies solemnly, and we can almost see the words, *Et in Arcadia ego*. Later in the film, this nostalgia is invoked visually, by a painting of prancing circus ponies shown hanging above Papa Mélé's bed at the moment of his death. These scenes serve to reinforce the circus's status as a waning form of community and thus as a marker of loss.

The film's depiction of another site of communal expression, the *bal populaire*, presents a further contrast with the music hall.[1] Ginette Vincendeau has noted that "French indigenous forms of popular dance (*java, valse musette*) are highly ritualized and strictly communal forms which do not allow for the virtuoso solos or duets of, say, flamenco, tango or American tap-dance and other related dances based on jazz music. French dance forms in the 1930s are represented mainly in populist films, in episodes designed to stress the spirit of a community rather than the performance of the dance itself" (1985, 143). Vincendeau includes *Zouzou* in her list of examples, along with Clair's *Le Quatorze juillet* and *Sous les toits de Paris*, Duvivier's *La Belle équipe*, Carné's *Hôtel du Nord*, and Renoir's *La Bête humaine*. I believe, however, that *Zouzou* stands apart from these films precisely because it combines communal dance with Hollywood showstoppers, reserving the latter for Zouzou, a West Indian, while excluding her from the former (although Zouzou accompanies Jean and Claire, her friendly rival for Jean's affections, to the *bal*, she herself does not dance). Zouzou's dancing is strictly performative, even within what would ordinarily be the communal environment of the laundry, where she sings and dances around while her co-workers, having formed a diegetic audience, cheer her on. This movement of separation from the surrounding community finds its ultimate expression at the very end of the film, in the song of regret Zouzou sings from the confines of her gilded cage.

The transition from earlier popular forms to music hall is mirrored in Josephine Baker's move from the music hall to film (as well, to a less spectacular degree, as that of her costar Gabin, who, in 1934, just on the brink of superstardom, received second billing to Baker). *Zouzou* was written especially for the screen, and although its story of the music hall projects us into this theatrical milieu, the cinematic perspective transforms the theatrical experience. Moving behind the scenes, the camera breaks down the barrier separating audience from performers. By removing this barrier (and thus distinguishing itself from the theatrical medium it is depicting), however, film reproduces the very myth of community—what Andrew calls "the rhetoric of 'intimacy' and 'contact' " (23)—manufactured by the music hall itself to compensate for its departure from traditional forms.

This illusion of intimacy and contact was reinforced by the star system that blurred the boundary between Baker's work and her life. An interview in the September 27, 1934, issue of *Pour Vous* describes her in terms that inevitably recall the character she plays in *Zouzou*: "Interviewing Josephine Baker might seem easy at first. But in reality, this undertaking turns out to be full of challenges. No sooner have you put a question to the versatile actress, than she eludes you, flitting birdlike around the room, admiring herself in a mirror or cranking up the phonograph and starting to sing one of those wild and languorous songs that are her trademark." Baker herself apparently cultivated this rapprochement; at the end of the interview, she confides to the reporter (and to the reading public), "It all seems so real, so true, that I sometimes think it's my own life that's unfolding on the set" (George 1934, 7). Baker's own persona adds another narrative layer, another intertext, to the film, invoking the star system (and many of the stars) that the music hall and cinema had in common.

Perhaps the only music-hall performer to overshadow Baker was Mistinguett, whose own foray into sound film took place just two years after the release of *Zouzou*. Christian Jacque's *Rigolboche*, which appeared in 1936, stars Mistinguett in her first (and last) role in a sound film. Like Baker, Mistinguett was able to attract large audiences based on her status as a music-hall superstar in a film that culminated in an elaborate production number before a diegetic music-hall audience. The film opens in Dakar, from which Mistinguett, who plays a French *chanteuse* in a small club, is forced to flee because of a mishap. Once in France, she finds work as a singer in a shady nightclub, where she soon becomes a star; with the help of a wealthy admirer, she is able to purchase the nightclub and transform it into a music hall in which she is the main attraction, descending a giant staircase in a swirl of ostrich feathers. In both *Rigolboche* and *Zouzou*, the eponymous heroine has come to France from an overseas colony. Unlike Zouzou's migration, however, Rigolboche's marks a return to her native land. It is this difference that, despite all the other remarkable similarities between the two films, sets them apart. Rigolboche's music-hall triumph coincides with her acceptance in the community to which she has returned, whereas Zouzou's success, which is every bit as dazzling, only underscores her exclusion from that community. This distinction is reflected not only in the spatial organization of the final stage productions (sweeping, open staircase versus cage) but also in the title and affective force of the song each star sings: "Je suis de Paris" (I'm from Paris), affirms Rigolboche jubilantly, whereas Zouzou's stage persona sadly pines away for her "Haïti."

The importance of national identity that emerges when one compares *Rigolboche* and *Zouzou* is reflected in the industry that produced these films. Whereas other entertainment forms had fashioned communities based on distinctions within French society, film shifted the terms of differentiation to an international level. From its inception, film in France had served as the pretext for passionate assertions of national identity, from the attribution of credit for the invention of film (Lumière versus Edison) to the debate over the implications of sound technology (Abel 1988). It is the latter issue that proved the most polarizing in the context of international competition, particularly from the United States, which possessed the capital and distribution capabilities to dominate the market. In the 1930s, the "universal" cinema of the silent era was replaced by what has often been termed a Babel of conflicting specificities, production companies (usually American) financing multilingual versions of the same film. Henri Jeanson has described the international atmosphere of Hollywood's French colony, in which a foreign language, "le Paramount," was spoken (Vincendeau 1985, 35). In this context, silent film was perceived retrospectively by many to represent a golden era of French cultural influence. Richard Abel has written of the pointedly nationalist tone adopted by certain critics of the new technology: "Bardèche and Brasillach looked back nostalgically to those magical silent days of their youth—to what they would later call the legendary *chanson de geste* or national voice of the French silent cinema" (1988, 150).

Contrary to the fears expressed by such critics, however, the French film industry really came into its own only after the advent of sound, as it accrued the cultural capital that would, by the end of the 1930s, make up for its lack of financial capital (Andrew 1995).

The anxiety that accompanied the advent of sound and the attendant nostalgia for the silent era that so dominated discussions about film in the early 1930s find expression in *Zouzou* in a number of ways. Near the beginning of the film, when Zouzou and Jean are children, Papa Mélé recalls the dying words of their respective fathers. After hearing the last words of Jean's father ("He told me—listen up—'I could only be his father, but you can be his papa' "), Zouzou asks, "And what did mine say?" Papa Mélé replies, "Well, yours told me the same thing, only with his eyes, the poor thing, because he could no longer speak." In the midst of this tender scene, we can see the painted portrait of a black-skinned clown on the wall in the background, the departed father. For although both children's fathers are absent, it is Zouzou's father whose absence is invoked later in the film (in the scene in which she pretends to be a clown). In this context, the dying clown's failure to impart final words is significant: his silence speaks to us, telling of the loss of an idealized little community, a family.

Conversely, images of sound in *Zouzou*—that is, moments in which sound itself is thematized—effectively convey discord, disruption, and dissonance. In one sequence, for example, three scenes are linked by means of a telephone, an object that will reappear in oversized form in the final production number. In the first of these scenes, one of the producers of the revue in which Zouzou will end up starring waits to use a telephone backstage at the music hall. Impatient, he screams at the woman on the phone, who drops the receiver and flees. We then cut to a ringing telephone in the bedroom of Miss Barbara, the starlet who has failed to show up for rehearsal. She answers the phone, assures the producer that she is on her way, and then begins to argue with her Brazilian lover. The phone rings again and the Brazilian answers; Barbara grabs the receiver and yells into it. The scene then shifts to a telephone at the laundry, where Claire's mother, the owner, is shown arguing with a customer. In all three of these scenes, the telephone, and thus the voice that it serves to project, is a site of discord, a source of intrusion.

It is in this context that the deafness of one of the music hall's producers, Saint-Lévy, can best be understood. His impairment forces those around him to shout; as the cause of excessive speech, he is the flipside of Zouzou's mute father. Saint-Lévy is coded as Jewish, his hybridized

Figure 7. *The big telephone number. Courtesy Bibliothèque du Film, Paris. All rights reserved.*

name the sign of an imperfect assimilation. Near the end of the film, as Zouzou's mad rush to make her scene on time creates chaos backstage, Saint-Lévy and an elderly seamstress nearly collapse from nervous exhaustion. When the seamstress comments that she has never seen such excitement in her thirty years at the music hall, Saint-Lévy adds that he has needed to be there only thirty days to see such excitement. His remark reinforces the stereotypical depiction of Jews as perpetual outsiders, an image that came to be interpreted literally in the French film industry (Hayward 1993, 153–55). In the 1930s, Jews were fired from production companies as the result of mounting antisemitism, fanned by the likes of, among others, Paul Morand—whose 1934 *France la doulce*, an antisemitic satire of the industry, would help get him appointed to head the bureau of film censorship under Vichy—and François Vinneuil / Lucien Rebatet, who argued that the French film industry should be purged of Jews and foreigners. The combined force of Saint-Lévy's Jewish identity and his association with exaggerated sound thus exemplifies Alice Kaplan's observation that "interest in a French national voice [was]

. . . constructed with the help of this notion of an encroaching foreign one" (1986, 134).

Foreignness and the voice are further linked in *Zouzou* by the preponderance of non-French accents: Miss Barbara's thick accent—which is unidentified but sounds eastern European—is in large part responsible for her massacre of the song she is supposed to sing in the revue: as her name suggests, there is something of the barbarian in her, someone who babbles nonsensically. She is shown to be as ineffectual in the music hall as those non-French silent film stars whose careers dissolved with the advent of sound film. Significantly, her biggest supporter is Saint-Lévy, whose deafness—as well, perhaps, as his own status as an outsider— renders him blissfully unaware of her accent or her false notes. Miss Barbara's eventual flight to Rio de Janeiro with her heavily accented Brazilian lover suggests that there is no place for this kind of alterity in France. The other character in the film whose French is accented is Zouzou, whose Martinican inflections bear a suspicious resemblance to Baker's own American accent. The respective fates of Miss Barbara and Zouzou prefigure the two alternatives facing immigrants at the end of the Third Republic and beyond: outright expulsion (as, for example, with the Jews in World War II) or the colonial (and postcolonial) policy of exclusion from within figured in Zouzou's enclosure within a cage at the end of the film.

I return below to the latter alternative; for now, it must suffice to signal the presence of a certain anxiety surrounding sound even in a film that was, after all, a musical and thus owed its success in large part to the sound revolution.[2] This ambivalence toward sound is reflected synecdochically in an extremely enigmatic moment in the film. After a scene in which Zouzou, having come to the dock to meet Jean, a sailor, learns that he has been confined to his ship for disciplinary reasons, we see a dark frame, with nothing visible but the white capital letters "LA" on the side of a ship, which stand out in stark contrast to the night sky and black ocean. This frame lingers for several seconds before yielding to the next scene, in which Jean is shown slipping off the ship and into the water, on his way to the humble flat shared by Zouzou and Papa Mélé. The white letters, apparently a definite article in the ship's name, draw the eye; they seem mysterious and certainly out of place. I suggest that this image can be read as an intertitle and, consequently, as an intertextual reference to silent film. Yet at the same time, this intertextuality is undermined by the word's multiple denotations. First of all, the letters combine to form the deictic "là," a sign that refers to referentiality itself (this reading of the word is echoed in the first thing we hear after it fades from view, when Zouzou, responding to Jean's knock at the door, says, "Qui est là? [Who is there?]"). By definition, a deictic must point to something beside(s) itself—yet, in the frame that shows us only the word "LA," all is darkness; as Gertrude Stein once said, there is no "there" there. So although the ghost of the silent era returns to haunt the film for a brief moment, it is paralyzed by its inability to refer to anything other than itself. If we read the letters in yet another light, however, their referential potential may be restored: as "la," a musical note, the letters evoke both Zouzou's gift for song and the very sound revolution that makes a movie musical such as this one possible. This moment of unconscious nostalgia for its own prehistory, which occurs in a film that appeared at a transitional period in the history of cinema, thus underscores the ambivalence of the industry toward the coming of sound. Although greeted by many with hostility, sound eventually led to the creation of a French national cinema (whose triumphs were nonetheless threatened by those of another national cinema based in Los Angeles, a city commonly referred to as "L.A.").

Whitewashing History

In *Imagined Communities*, Benedict Anderson writes of the role of mechanical reproduction in creating new modes of community: "Print-capitalism . . . made it possible for rapidly growing numbers of people to think about themselves, and to relate themselves to others, in profoundly new ways" (Anderson 1993, 36). An imagined community, he explains, is any community "larger than primordial villages of face-to-face contact" (6). In *Zouzou*, such an imagined community is represented by the newspapers circulating throughout the film and is contrasted with another community, that of the laundry workers in the *blanchisserie* where Zouzou is employed before becoming a music-hall star.

This contrast is emphasized thematically, in a number of scenes that juxtapose laundry and newspapers. In the first scene to take place in the laundry, for example, the workers are shown "reading" the undergarments of their customers as if they were newspapers, holding them up, identifying their owners, and speculating about their financial status and romantic adventures: "In this business, you end up getting to know all the dirt [*dessous*; literally, underthings], because you have to iron it out!" Conversely, in an earlier scene, Zouzou uses a newspaper to dry a pan, as if the paper were a piece of linen; it is in the same paper, in a want ad, that she then learns of the opening at the laundry. Finally, in the most explicit juxtaposition, a printing press turning out hundreds of newspapers dissolves to a shot of a laundry press rolling out a piece of linen. The purpose of this repeated coupling, I believe, is to construct a community based on the face-to-face contact of which Anderson speaks and which is coded as authentic in opposition to an imagined one. As a measure of its authenticity, this community even includes the mother figure that is otherwise absent in the film, Mme Vallée, Claire's mother and owner of the laundry. The camaraderie among the female laundry workers serves as a counterpoint to the scenes of male bonding so prevalent in French films of the 1930s—yet even this community is marked by the absence of a father, an absence inscribed in the very name of the shop, La Veuve Vallée (The Widow Vallée). The fact that the community is composed entirely of women underscores its homogeneity, here represented by, but not limited to, the criterion of gender. So, for example, the laundry workers sing in unison as they iron, but they stop singing when Zouzou comes in, because she can sing *for* them but not *with* them. For although Zouzou seems to be one of the girls, she is marked by a difference that prevents her from being absorbed into their community, a difference that can be summed up in part by Homi Bhabha's characterization of the "assimilated" colonial identity: "Almost the same but not quite. . . . Almost the same but not white" (1994, 322). Despite her attempt to become a *blanchisseuse*, one who whitens, Zouzou still loses the object of her affections to a woman named Claire (clear, light in color).

A scene that takes place early in the film quite literally illustrates the nature of Zouzou's difference from those around her. Jean has just returned from his year-long naval duty; while bantering with him, Zouzou notices a tattoo of a woman on his arm. "Who is that woman?" she asks jealously. "Oh," Jean says, "anyone [*n'importe laquelle*]." Clearly upset, Zouzou scowls and moves away from him. This is the first time in the film that her expression has betrayed anything other than unbridled joy. She apparently realizes what the film's plot will bear out, namely, that Jean is not quite right when he says that the woman outlined in ink can be any woman at all. She must be a woman whose flesh is the color of his own arm. Although the imagined community of *la plus grande France*, the colonial empire that was to comprise "100 million Frenchmen" from all corners of the globe, is predicated on a symbolic identity, a hypothetical substitutability, among all its members (the "n'importe laquelle" tattooed on Jean's arm), the perception of visible (or, as the function of accents in the film shows, audible) difference disrupts the assimilation

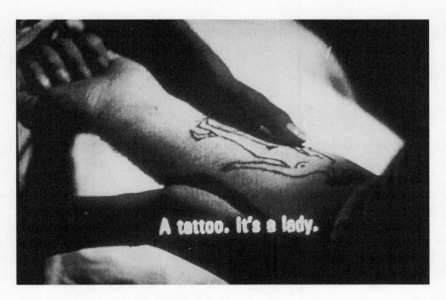

A tattoo. It's a lady.

Figure 8. *Jean shows Zouzou his tattoo. Frame enlargement.*

process. Although Jean claims, when asked, that he cannot think of Zouzou in a romantic light because she is like a sister to him, it turns out that such excessive similarity actually masks excessive difference.[3]

It is in light of this difference that the film's insistence on doubles and multiple images must be read (a doubling that is itself mirrored aurally, or echoed, in the proliferation of double-phonemed names throughout the film: Zouzou, Papa, Barbara, Mimi, and "Fifine" in the song Jean sings while dancing with Claire at the *bal*). First, we see the child Zouzou's triple reflection in a vanity mirror as she powders her face; then, in the famous spotlight scene, her shadow is projected onto the curtain behind her as she prances around backstage; and finally, in the film's penultimate scene, a distraught Zouzou, rejected by Jean, passes a wall displaying several publicity posters of herself. (This multiplication of Zouzou's image was prefigured in two of the dance numbers in which Baker appeared in 1926 and 1927 at the Folies Bergère. In one, she danced the Charleston on a mirror that refracted her shadow across the stage, and in another, she danced the Black Bottom in front of a screen on which was projected a film of her doing the same dance [Kear 1996, 62 and 64].) In *Zouzou*, such multiple images are so many visual metaphors

Figure 9. *A dejected Zouzou walks past posters of herself. Frame enlargement.*

of an impossible assimilation. For example, the posters bearing Zouzou's likeness only underscore the cruel irony of her situation, her isolation and abandonment. Similarly, the face that she admires narcissistically in the early scene at the vanity mirror has been whitened with powder stolen from a white woman, who yells at her and chases her away. When we reach the spotlight scene, Zouzou has just encouraged a group of dancers to pat powder all over her body: "Faites-moi belle [Make me beautiful]" she says, and although the white light of France's *mission civilisatrice* is projected onto her (significantly, by Jean, a white Frenchman), the shadow it casts appears all the darker. In this context, the soldierly pose Baker strikes repeatedly in this scene, its impact augmented by the great span of her outstretched arms and legs, invokes the *tirailleur sénégalais*, the *zouave (native colonial soldier)* in which the name Zouzou originates. Like the silhouette that appears against the curtain as Zouzou dances before the spotlight, the Enlightenment ideal of universalism proves to be the self projected onto the world.

Yet the world was changing. It is no accident that in the caged-bird song, Zouzou's native Martinique, still yoked to France, is replaced by Haiti, lost long ago. The interwar period marked the beginning of the end of France's colonial empire: the apogee, the apotheosis of *la plus grande France* was also its swan song. So, too, with the proliferation of *bals populaires* at the very moment that such popular forms of communal expression were threatened with extinction by the music halls, which in turn would be converted into movie palaces (what better name, then, for the *bal* that Zouzou, Claire, and Jean frequent than Chez Oscar?). Yet, despite the fact that it was the wave of the future, film contained within it the seeds of the past. As Zouzou and the film bearing her name traverse the distance between circus and music hall, intimacy and bereavement, to culminate in a scene that encapsulates that movement in a single musical image—Haiti—we realize that it is not only a lost love she mourns but also the end of an era.

Into the Melting Pot: Cooking and Cultural Influence in *Princesse Tam-Tam*

In *Zouzou*, the nostalgia for a supposedly uncorrupted era was reflected in the title character's wistful longing for her humble-but-happy existence prior to the lonely glamour of her music-hall stardom. Although Edmond Gréville's 1935 *Princesse Tam-Tam* echoes this nostalgia, the later film's depiction of its star's attempt to assimilate into French society takes a different turn: in her second talking (and singing) feature film, Baker's status as the uncivilized object of civilized cultural consumption is transferred to the big screen in a quite literal way.

In *Princesse Tam-Tam*, a jaded Parisian novelist, played by Albert Préjean, travels to Tunisia for inspiration. There he encounters the shepherdess Alwina, played by Baker, whom he decides to bring back to France in order to observe the ensuing civilizing process and record it in his latest novel. Alwina's first lesson in civilization sets the stage for all those to come: after marveling that the French are able to discipline their appetites to correspond with mealtimes, she is told, "A stomach can be civilized." Alwina's attempted cultural assimilation is thus inaugurated by an image of biological assimilation: digestion. This scene depicts only one of a series of gustatory and culinary metaphors that proliferate throughout the film, images of chemical and biological transformation (cooking and eating) that symbolize the process of cultural transformation, as we saw in Crevel's *Babylone*.

At the same time, the film thematizes, or represents, representation itself, as the transformation of experience into language. The civilizing of

Figure 10. *The big finale: Zouzou in her birdcage, singing "Haïti." Courtesy Bibliothèque du Film, Paris. All rights reserved.*

Alwina's stomach, and of the rest of her, is, after all, performed for the purpose of representing the whole process in a book (or so it seems; we learn at the end of the film that Alwina's metamorphosis has been imagined by the writer, whose documentary pretensions turn out to be a literary conceit, his "true account" nothing more than a novel). Both kinds of transformation, the civilizing process and the art of representation, are treated in the film as forms of corruption and are depicted with equal contempt: the last scene shows the novelist's completed work, aptly titled *Civilisation*, being eaten by a donkey.

In the context of this cinematic Pygmalion story, the metamorphoses wrought by cooking and eating symbolize the transformation of a natural state in the cultural sphere, of a corruption, in other words, of cultural origins—much as the name Baker evokes a *boulanger* in foreign disguise. Produced in the aftermath of the 1934 antiparliamentary riots, *Princesse Tam-Tam* raised questions of national identity in an era of growing xenophobia. Encounters with cultural differences at home, in the form of immigration, and abroad, in the form of colonialism (Tunisia, in which much of the film is set, was a French protectorate from 1881 until its independence in 1956), were playing an increasingly important role in French cultural life. As Alwina adjusts her appetite to the sound of the dinner bell, the film suggests, she assimilates into French society, committing the double crime of abandoning her native Tunisia—depicted as a pastoral idyll—and rendering ever more impure the culture she attempts to adopt. Yet, despite its encyclopedic range of images—from Paris burlesque to the mysterious Orient, from African drumbeats to Busby Berkeley–inspired dance numbers—*Princesse Tam-Tam* does not place all its cultural signifiers on an equal footing. Just as no encyclopedia, even the most ambitious, could be truly all-inclusive without succumbing to the exigencies of selection and hierarchy, so the Enlightenment concept of assimilation presupposes a "natural" hierarchy of civilizing forces. Ultimately, the film's hodgepodge of cultural signifiers, its melting pot of Orientalist and Africanist discourses, privileges the preservation of boundaries that the rhetoric of exoticism would seem to negate.

Pastoral Pleasures

In its opening sequences, *Princesse Tam-Tam* establishes a stark dichotomy between the decadence of life in the Parisian fast lane and the pastoral innocence of the Tunisian *bled*, or rural outback. With the credits still rolling, shots of the magnificent Roman ruins of Dougga dissolve into one another. The scene then shifts to the film's first diegetic setting, in the tension-filled home of the novelist Max de Mirecourt and his wife, Lucie, who are shown squabbling bitterly. This scene of domestic discord contrasts sharply with the preceding image of bucolic tranquillity. In the midst of the couple's hostile exchange over the woman's flirtation with a wealthy Indian maharajah, the novelist's assistant, Coton, enters,

Figure 11. *Alwina playing among the ruins of Dougga in* Princesse Tam-Tam. *Courtesy Bibliothèque du Film, Paris. All rights reserved.*

and the two men discuss Mirecourt's need for a change of scenery. Contemplating images painted on his wallpaper of palm trees and a Middle Eastern shepherd, the novelist, suddenly inspired, cries: "We'll go where the savages are! Real savages! That's right, to Africa!" The scene then shifts to an exterior location, shot in Tunisia, where a shepherdess (Baker) frolics in the natural setting, nuzzling affectionately with sheep and prancing across the *bled*.

The contrast between the two lifestyles—the decadence of the Parisian bourgeoisie and the innocent charm of rural Tunisian life—could not be more explicit. Yet the very ruins that provide the backdrop for this pastoral idyll also signal decay, serving as a literal reminder of the ruin that befell the Roman empire when it extended too far beyond its borders. When the novelist and a group of snooty French tourists visit the site on their rented camels, they are clearly interlopers, bringing such modern and incongruous amenities as a phonograph with them. The dichotomy between the cynical French tourists (on seeing the shepherdess, one woman remarks, "I can see that you like nature, but isn't this a bit much?") and the pastoral setting suggests that these decadent, world-weary French have strayed far from the innocence of civilization's origins. The shepherdess's name, Alwina, we are told, means "petite source" (both little stream and little source), and it is apparent that the French tourists have little in common with this source. Appropriately, the scene depicting the penetration of the French into the ruins is introduced by a wipe, a filmic technique in which a line sweeps across the screen, seeming to pull a new scene into view as it pushes the previous one out of the picture. This technique, at its height of popularity in 1935 and used unsparingly in *Princesse Tam-Tam*, illustrates the replacement of the past by the present, showing new scenes, like new empires, pushing aside the old.

It is at the foot of the Roman ruins that Alwina performs a trick that endears her to Mirecourt (who, as a detached observer of the group of French tourists to which he belongs, reverses the anthropologist's role of participant-observer). While the unsuspecting tourists eat their lunch, Alwina empties the salt from its shaker and replaces it with dirt. When the tourists grimace in horror after biting into their liberally "salted" eggs, the novelist, who has observed the whole scene, bursts into laughter. Alwina thus gets the better of the tourists by disrupting their highly orchestrated dining ritual. Likewise, the scene opens with a parallel-action sequence, cross-cutting between a group of Tunisian children tearing hungrily into hunks of bread and a shot of the French using polished silver utensils to poke daintily at little plates of poached egg. The contrast established is that between a way of eating depicted as "natural" and a way of eating that is highly mediated by the conventions of civilized society. In fact, the writer's first encounter with Alwina involves food: he and Coton are sitting in a café when he notices her stealing an orange from a tray momentarily set down by a waiter; the writer buys the whole tray of fruit for her, and she gleefully runs off with it. Food is a marker of degrees of civilization even in its mode of distribution: by stealing the orange, Alwina shows herself to be outside the socialized circuit of exchange; by buying it for her, by legitimating the transaction, Mirecourt initiates the process that will bring her within the bounds of civilized society.

It is significant that the contrasting culinary practices described above are exercised in the shadow of the ruins of imperial Rome. This juxtaposition evokes the Enlightenment view that the fall of the Roman empire could be attributed, at least in part, to its cooking habits. According to the article titled "Gourmandise" in the *Encyclopédie*, "The Romans collapsed beneath the weight of their grandeur, moderation became the object of scorn, and the frugality of Curius and Fabricius gave way to the sensuality of Catius and Apicius" (Diderot and d'Alembert 1966, 7:754). But just what is it that brought about this change in eating habits? Where did it come from? The seeds of decline, it seems, were imported from Asia:

> Delicacy of the table passed from Asia to the other peoples of the Earth. The Persians communicated to the Greeks this branch of luxury, which the wise legislators of Lacedaemonia resisted with all their might.
>
> The Romans, having become rich and impotent, shook off their former laws, abandoned their frugal lifestyle, and tasted the high life. . . . This was merely the first step toward sensuality of the table, which they soon pushed to the highest degree of expense and corruption. (Le Chevalier de Jaucourt, "Cuisine," in Diderot and d'Alembert 1966, 4:537)

French culinary treatises published in the interwar period follow in the tradition established by the Encyclopédistes. After declaring, in *Les Plaisirs de la table*, that "hors-d'oeuvres originated in Asia," Édouard Nignon explains, "In France, hors-d'oeuvres have always held little interest for true eaters, who regard them as a veritable pleonasm, a superfluous addition to a well-cooked meal" (Nignon 1926, 20). Nignon thus reinforces the idea that the Orient brought decadent excess to France. In another work, published in 1933, the author warns young chefs of the dangers of foreign influences: "Beware exotic dishes, which destroy our gastronomic harmony; their coarse sauces and raging spices, suited to stimulate lazy stomachs tired out by the heat, are not destined for the palate of a gourmet" (Nignon 1933, 36). In the view of the Encyclopédistes, imperial Rome could have benefited from such warnings—proferred, alas, too late—when, by mingling with other cultures, by letting its borders become too elastic, it opened itself up to the corruption that led to its downfall. Twentieth-century France, on the other hand, had overcome this temptation, according, at any rate, to a modern-day descendant of the literary genre originated by Diderot. The 1928 *Larousse du XXe siècle* manages to cast a xenophobic light on French culinary heritage when, without providing any indication of a departure from the subject of French tradition, the article titled "Cuisine" suddenly announces, "The beginning of the twentieth century was marked, moreover, by a return to the healthful [*saine*] French tradition, and while there exist in France establishments that offer various exotic cuisines, most establishments . . . , mindful of their reputation, have gone to great lengths

to offer their clientele nothing but the choicest dishes [*mets de choix*]"
(*Larousse du XXe siècle* 1928 2:614). Words such as "saine" and "mets de choix" here oppose French cuisine to an unhealthy, undesirable "cuisine exotique."

Neither the Encyclopédistes (of the twentieth or the eighteenth century) nor *Princesse Tam-Tam* suggests that cooking as such corrupts; rather, it is excess in cooking, or excessive cooking, that produces too much of a good thing. In the transition from nature to culture, the danger is that one will go too far, transforming the savage into the overly civilized. This stage, on the continuum that includes the raw and the cooked, is what Claude Lévi-Strauss calls the *"plus-que-cuit"* (more-than-cooked) (1964, 406). The *"plus-que-cuit"* is a culturally mediated form of excess, as opposed to the rotten, which is a natural process of degradation from within. For Lévi-Strauss, the *plus-que-cuit* is both effected and represented by smoke—an image relentlessly associated, in *Princesse Tam-Tam,* with the maharajah who flirts with the novelist's wife. Smoke is also associated, albeit to a lesser degree, with the novelist, who is often shown smoking, as if to suggest that the cultural "overdoneness," the sense of overwrought civilization from which the novelist suffers, was imported from the East, from the Asia that also brought worldwide gastronomic corruption.

If there is any figure in the film who represents unbridled extravagance and excess, or overdoneness, it is the maharajah. His great wealth is mentioned often, and he is always shown in ornately luxurious surroundings. It is to him that the novelist's wife runs when she wishes to indulge her own decadence; it is only when she leaves the maharajah at the end of the film that conjugal harmony is restored. As if to confirm this image of excess, the maharajah is often enveloped in a cloud of smoke, which is shown either curling in tendrils from his exaggeratedly long cigarette holder or rising from the enormous incense burner that dominates his private apartments. When the actress who plays the novelist's wife, Germaine Aussay, appears in her opening credit, she too is shown puffing languorously on a cigarette, prefiguring her flirtatious association with the maharajah's corrupting influence.

Rather than signify the East per se, however, smoke in the film points to the corruption wrought by cultural influence. The smoke that represents the crossing of cultural boundaries is thus shown rising from a ship's smokestack, to signify a *traversée*, a literal crossing that brings Alwina closer to the foreign land that will, in the space of the film's story-within-a-story, transform her and be transformed by her. And when Al-

Figure 12. *Alwina, learning to be a lady. Courtesy Bibliothèque du Film, Paris. All rights reserved.*

wina, having been manicured, dressed, polished, and instructed in the civilizing arts of music and multiplication tables, makes her grand entrance before Mirecourt and Coton, the camera lingers on an image of a monkey smoking a cigarette painted on the door that separates her from her mentors, literally marking the threshold that divides Alwina from the side of civilization. The implication is that fancy clothes and refined social graces are as ridiculous on a North African as is a cigarette in the

Figure 13. *The maharajah with Alwina. Courtesy Bibliothèque du Film, Paris. All rights reserved.*

hands of a monkey. But the cigarette also reinforces the film's association between smoke and an excess of civilization—which is to say, the adoption of a culture not originally one's "own."

Positioned at the opposite end of the culinary spectrum, images of rawness and unmediated consumption in the film suggest a state of nature unaffected by modern life. When the novelist's assistant goes to fetch Alwina, whom he will deceptively present to the press as a princess from the mythical country of Parador, she is shown greedily stuffing couscous into her face without inhibition, and without eating utensils. This scene indicates that she still has a long way to go in the civilizing process and remains to a large extent in the "raw" state in which the novelist found her (since the couscous appears to have been boiled, the implication is that Alwina has nonetheless been civilized a bit—although Lévi-Strauss notes that some cultures consider boiling to be the least culturally mediated form of cooking because the end result resembles the natural process of rotting [Lévi-Strauss 1964, 406]). Thus, when we see Alwina vigorously sucking a large piece of raw fruit at the end of

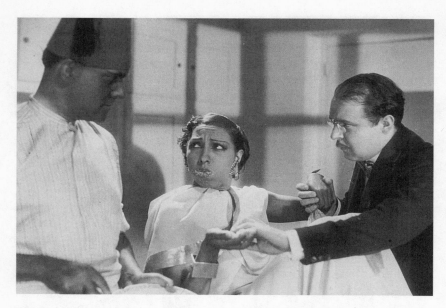

Figure 14. *Alwina enjoys a snack. Courtesy Bibliothèque du Film, Paris. All rights reserved.*

the film, we know that she has not been civilized after all. As the "little source" of Alwina's name suggests, this is eating in its pure form.

Corruption, then, is synonymous with straying from the source, be it cultural or culinary. As forms of cooking strayed from their geographical sources, they also strayed from the source of the food being prepared: according to the Encyclopédistes, who refer to cooking as "cet art trompeur" (that art of deception) and to cooks as "artistes en cuisine," cooking became corrupt when it began dabbling in the art of deception. Cooks wanted nothing more than to "change the appearance of all the morsels they wished to prepare; they imitated the fish that were coveted but unavailable, by giving other fish the same taste and shape as those that were out of season. Trimalcion's cook even used fish meat to create different animals, such as wood-pigeons, turtle doves, fat pullets, etc." This creative cookery was also described as the act of "disfiguring in a hundred different ways the foods that nature provides" (Diderot and d'Alembert 1966, 4:538). Cooking is corrupt because it disguises its raw materials by means of artifice, making one thing look like another, as Alwina is made to look like a princess.

Indeed, civilization is equated in *Princesse Tam-Tam* with deception. When the novelist's assistant declares, speaking of Alwina at the beginning of the film, "We must civilize her," and the novelist complains, "But I don't know how to go about it," the assistant replies knowingly, "Teach her to lie." For Alwina, assimilation is tantamount to dissimulation. When she is first shown her room in Paris, the camera alights successively on the artificial flowers, fish, and birds in the room as if viewing them through her eyes. We see Alwina's astonished expression in a reaction shot, as she marvels, "It's funny how many false things there are here." The novelist replies, "You know, so many false things are more beautiful than the real thing." The film, of course, belies this notion; Alwina's is the voice of naive reason. Blatant artifice pervades the film, a caveat for modern society, from the artificial palm trees that adorn Alwina's windowsill, shown through the iron grill that suggests her sad imprisonment, to the large artificial flowers that trim the neckline on Lucie's dress as she visits the maharajah, primed for decadent, unnatural deeds.

But the filmic image that says the most about the relation between artifice and nature is a sequence that takes place when Alwina is posing as the princess of Parador. In this sequence, which begins at the racetrack where Alwina, sporting a formal riding costume and top hat, watches the races, the scene shifts from more to progressively less mimetic forms of representation. As Alwina views the horse race directly, without the aid of any ocular apparatus, several spectators are shown looking through binoculars, including Coton, whose binoculars get comically tangled up in his eyeglasses; then a vertical wipe shifts the scene to a painting of Alwina with a horse, hanging in a gallery as passersby admire it. The scene then changes to an exterior shot in which Alwina checks her makeup in a compact mirror, as a photographer captures the moment on film; then there is a cut to a sculpture of Alwina's head; then a dissolve to a realistic drawing of her face, which is followed by a montage of increasingly exaggerated caricatures of her, after which the sculpture appears again. As the sequence ends, the shot of the sculpture dissolves to a closeup of the artificial palm trees that adorn the window of her bedroom, where Alwina sits forlornly, listening to Middle Eastern music on the radio, until a stern male voice booms: "Our Oriental music program has ended. We now return to the most recent figures from the stock exchange." The relentless succession of what might be called, after John Berger, ways of seeing, accompanies Alwina's assimilation into French culture. The progression (or declension) from unaided vision to eyeglasses to binoculars, realistic painting, mirror, photograph, and sculpture, to drawings that become increasingly distorted, suggests that the Westernized Alwina has strayed from the authentic Alwina. The caricature sequence occurs at the very zenith of her assimilation, when she is being feted and fawned over at the racetrack in her incarnation as a high-society woman (prefiguring Eliza Doolittle's apotheosis, also at a racetrack, in the film *My Fair Lady*). The increasingly distorted caricatures misrepresent Alwina much as she misrepresents herself; the implication seems to be that, in all her genteel finery, Alwina is as grotesque and unnatural as the clownish cartoons purporting to depict her (or as a monkey smoking a cigarette).

The issue of representation, made explicit in the racetrack sequence, raises the question of Mirecourt's book, which provides both the pretext and the narrative frame for the film's plot. This book, which begins the film as a record of Alwina's assimilation, is eventually revealed to be a fictional account of an assimilation that has occurred only in the novelist's imagination: what started out as false fiction (because a true document) turns out to be true fiction (a false document). The interplay between these forms of representation—fictional and documentary—mirrors the conflict between two modes of representing the exotic, known respectively as Orientalism and Africanist discourse.

Orientalism and Africanist Discourse

Princesse Tam-Tam begins with a bewildering juxtaposition of Africanist and Orientalist signifiers. The film's opening credits roll to the tune of Middle Eastern–style music laced with percussion that evokes a (sub-Saharan) tom-tom. When Baker's credit, along with a closeup of her face, appears, she is wearing a headdress that is reminiscent of ancient Egyptian pharaohs, and earrings shaped like pyramids; yet, when the film's title appears soon after this, it is over a shot of a black African man beating a bongo drum and singing, his words and music drowned out by the nondiegetic soundtrack. Thus the film sets up musically and visually its underlying cultural confusion between Orientalism and Africanist discourses. This confusion is evident when, for example, Alwina, disguised as a visiting dignitary, is described as a "princesse noire" by the novelist's wife, whereas in the next scene, Mirecourt and Coton boast to the press that the mysterious princess's father is the king of a central Indian tribe. Other than the film's title and the image of the black African drummer, which does not recur until late in the film (and then for only a split second between shots during the big dance-production number), the only sign of Africanness is Josephine Baker's own public identity as a woman of African descent. But although the Orientalist images dominate the film on a narrative level, it is the Africanist discourse that prevails on an ideological one.

The distinctions between Orientalism and Africanist discourse have often been blurred in generalizations about the exotic. Orientalism is the term Edward Said uses to denote the Western quest for the accumulation of knowledge about peoples deemed exotic, the academic pretense of an objective, scientific ordering of data that are taken to reflect a given reality (Said 1979). Africanist discourse, in contrast, is described by Christopher Miller as "the collapse of knowledge" (Miller 1985, 23 and 246), an avowedly creative impulse that fills in the gaps it creates with images drawn from fantasy. In Africanist discourse, writes Miller, "the blank slate of Africa, with no past or future, can be made to fulfill the desires of your own present" (248). The confusion between the strains of exoticism that weave through *Princesse Tam-Tam* is not unconnected to this opposition: on the one hand, images of the Orient evoke the pretense of recording Alwina's transformation in a document; on the other hand, images of Africa reinforce the revelation that the whole story is, after all, a work of fiction. As the novelist's documentary stance turns out to be composed of fantasy, so Orientalism's claim to impartial observation and the recording of facts can be said to consist largely of stereotypes based in fantasy, as flat and two-dimensional as the cartoons of Middle Eastern shepherds and palm trees painted on the wallpaper in the novelist's Parisian apartment.

It is in this context that we can best understand the scene in which the maharajah, showing off his butterfly collection (the Oriental as Orientalist), visualizes a butterfly in the blank space he has reserved for his next romantic conquest, the novelist's wife: the image of the phantom butterfly fading in and out evokes an analogous filling-in of blanks in knowledge with the stuff of fantasy. Likewise, the shedding of the documentary pretense at the end of the film in favor of fiction suggests that Orientalism is giving way to Africanist discourse, much as Alwina finally sheds her Paradorian persona (as well as her evening gown) and succumbs to the beat of the tom-tom at the maharajah's gala party. Baker herself described the film's plot as "the story of an Arab urchin who is transformed into a social butterfly by a French nobleman" (Baker and Chase 1993, 187). Baker's account, however, overlooks the fact that in the end, Alwina does not become a social butterfly after all; assimilation is shown to be a fantasy that will fade as surely as the imagined butterfly in the maharajah's collection. Similarly, a scene in which Coton attempts to imitate the Chinese plate spinners who number among the entertainers at the maharajah's party (evoking both culinary and Orientalist motifs) suggests that what works for one culture does not work for another: Coton's plate spins out of control, implying that imitation is a bad idea. The film, finally, favors retaining the distance, mystery, and myth that result from the maintenance of the physical and ideological boundaries that separate cultures.

The Ruins of the Third Republic

Princesse Tam-Tam tells not one but two Pygmalion stories: Alwina is not only impersonating a Westerner; she is also impersonating a princess. In a reversal of the archetypal pastoral story of *Daphnis and Chloe*, in which royals disguise themselves as simple country folk, Alwina's humble origins are concealed beneath the trappings of a princess. The *guinguette*, a riverside, working-class bar to which Alwina flees when she has had enough of high society, is the only place she feels at home. When she is mobbed by admiring partygoers after the big dance number, in which she has succumbed to the beat of the tom-tom and danced frenetically in front of the guests at the maharajah's toney gala, it is precisely for her exotic appeal, for her inability to fit in, that she is appreciated. As if to reinforce this idea, in a subsequent scene the maharajah urges her to go back where she came from, suggesting an affinity between them based on their status as exotic outsiders: "I could have told all those people who you really were."

The film seems to present a utopian vision of the working class, along the lines of, for example, Renoir's *Le Crime de Monsieur Lange*. When Alwina is on her way out the door for a night on the town with her Tunisian beau Tahar after turning down an embassy dinner with Mirecourt, she says that she wants to go "into the crowd with people who know how to have a good time on their own terms, who can say and do whatever they want!" The carefree lifestyle of the working class appears to be glorified in much the same way as the insouciance of life on the Tunisian (or Indian, or "Paradorian") *bled*. When Lucie's aristocratic friends drop by for the local color, recalling Marie Antoinette in her shepherdess outfit, they are shocked to see Alwina singing and dancing joyously, in a manner, apparently, unbecoming a princess, even a "princesse noire." Conversely, the idea that members of the working class can "say and do whatever they want" suggests that the aristocratic novelist's cohorts are as inauthentic as the artificial flora and fauna that surround them.

Although, like Renoir's *La Règle du jeu*, *Princesse Tam-Tam* presents an indictment of aristocratic decadence in the twilight of the Third Republic, it is not necessary, or even useful, to reduce the film's colonial theme to a displacement of French class struggle. Rather than stand in for one another, the film's colonial politics and its class politics work together, because immigrants occupied and continue to occupy the lowest rungs of the socioeconomic ladder in France. (This collusion of class and racial barriers is illustrated in the following exchange: when Alwina expresses surprise after Mirecourt tells her that Coton, who in effect does his bidding, is his "slave," Coton adds, "I am a *nègre* [ghostwriter, but also 'Negro'], as you can see, my dear.") With immigration, the colonial question became inseparable from the question of class. Ultimately, the film preaches cultural separatism, whether it takes the form of an antidemocratic division of classes or an opposition to immigration.

Meanwhile, looming in the background of this story of failed assimilation are the ruins of Dougga, a stark reminder of the danger of crossing boundaries. This separatist ethic explains how the *Encyclopédie* could depict the Orient both as a bad influence, responsible, through the spread of its overwrought cooking, for the decline of the West ("Cuisine"), and, in "Gourmandise," as a pastoral paradise: "The freshness and ripe old age of the Persians and Chaldeans was a gift they owed to their barley bread and their fountain water" (Diderot and d'Alembert 1966, 7:754). It also explains how the maharajah, in a panegyric to the Orient that prefigures Alwina's identification with the working class, can exclaim: "The Orient is wonderful! Everyone is at one with nature. I know that you call us savages, but even the most miserable wretch among us has an independence you can't imagine." This contradiction seems to suggest that, when it is undisturbed, the Orient is wholesome, simple fare, but the crossing of borders brings trouble, causing it to become overdone. Both *Princesse Tam-Tam* and *Zouzou* would seem to celebrate a mixing of cultures, but they actually seek to preserve the exotic as such—that is, to keep it literally on the outside (*ex*).

For this is the film's lesson. We must stay within our own borders, even if what lies on the other side is nature itself, as the article "Gourmandise" in the *Encyclopédie* suggests: "Anything that goes beyond nature is useless and ordinarily harmful: one must not always follow even nature to where it would permit one to go; it is better to stay within the limits it has dictated for us, rather than pass beyond them" (7:754). Nature, suggests the *Encyclopédie*, is for the natural; it is Alwina, suggests the film, and not Mirecourt, who belongs on the *bled*. And this is where we find her as *Princesse Tam-Tam* draws to a close, having taken over the Tunisian villa formerly inhabited by the novelist, in a triumphant reversal of the march of Progress. As Alwina bounces a beautiful baby in her arms, in contrast to the apparently childless writer and his wife, her adoring husband Tahar shapes a clay pot on a kiln. The pot, an unadorned vessel, is not likely to be spun on an acrobat's stick in a stage show or sewn into a dancer's sequined costume; similarly, the luxurious villa, no longer the playground of the idle rich, has been converted to a barnyard. In the midst of such solid, uncorrupted values, a book called *Civilisation* serves its noblest purpose as a donkey's breakfast.

CHAPTER 5

꿋ᐱᕐ

Difference in Disguise

Paul Morand's Black Magic

La Terre cesse d'étre un drapeau aux couleurs violentes: c'est l'âge sale du métis.

Paul Morand, quoted in *Paul Morand: Le sourire du hara-kiri*, by
Pascal Louvrier and Eric Canal-Forgues

Like Josephine Baker, Paul Morand played a highly visible role in French culture of the interwar period; nevertheless, his work is largely overlooked today. In a reflection of the turbulent partnership between literature and politics in twentieth-century France, his canonical stature has waxed and waned according to the shifting parameters of political—and critical—correctness. One of the most popular writers of the 1920s and 1930s, Morand was praised by Céline as "le premier de nos écrivains qui *ait jazzé* la langue française" [the first of our writers *to jazz* the French language] (cited in Collomb 1993, 46); the neologism, in Céline's original emphasis, pointed as much to the jazz age in which and of which Morand wrote as to his use of language. More recently, Morand was hailed by Philippe Sollers in his preface to a paperback edition of Morand's *New York* as "the best French writer of the twentieth century, with the exception of Proust and Céline" (Morand 1988, 7). Yet Morand was ostracized after the Second World War for his allegiance to the Vichy regime, in which he served in Laval's cabinet and was for a time director of the bureau of film censorship and ambassador to Berne under Pétain. The writer's election to the Académie française in 1968 signaled a willingness on the part of the literary establishment to forgive his wartime indiscretions, but at the same time, it condemned him to the posthumous obscurity that typically befalls the (all-too-mortal) Immortals. In the 1990s, he enjoyed something of a resurgence, with the publication of a Pléiade edition of his short stories—the French canonical consecration par excellence—in 1992. This newfound legitimacy, though, seems to have entailed an obfuscation of the political dimension of Morand's work, and of its racial implications in particular. Manifestly a proponent of exoticism, a diplomat and travel writer known for his interest in other cultures, his condemnation of some forms of racism blinded critics to the implications of the cultural separatism he promoted.

It is perhaps because of this unwillingness to acknowledge Morand's ideological positions that one of his most popular—and polemical—short story collections of the interwar period, *Magie noire* (1928), has been virtually overlooked by later critics, who have been reluctant to hold Morand accountable for his racial politics. In 1992, Michel Collomb, editor of the Pléiade edition of the *Nouvelles complètes*, wrote, "A restless spirit not bound to ideas, Morand does not lock himself into a classic racist attitude; in his short stories can be found the echo of all the opinions competing with one another in his day, however mutually contradictory they might be" (Morand 1992, 1030). Collomb seems to suggest that Morand did not privilege one opinion over any other but acted merely as an impartial observer, a mirror reflecting any and all ideologies with which it came into contact. Similarly, Derayeh Derakhshesh contends that Morand did not place any one race above another, arguing that if Morand "rules out the possibility of assimilation," nonetheless "he never brings in preferential criteria; such an approach even brings him to praise the black instinct" (Derakhshesh 1990, 400). Morand's fascination with the exotic, his desire to preserve cultural differences, is seen to excuse his racism, as in this assessment by Marc Hanrez, which is not untypical: "His most inflammatory remarks, or at least those that appear so today, are always balanced by his favorable comments" (Collomb 1993, 51).

The most popular defense of Morand, however, seems to be that his work should be judged solely on aesthetic grounds. Stéphane Sarkany writes that "Morand's racism, however arbitrary it may be, is that of a moralist and an aesthete, not of an ideologue or a politician" (Sarkany 1968, 114). Ginette Guitard-Auviste, too, distinguishes between aesthetics and politics, arguing that it is useless to consider Morand's work from a social perspective, because it "has no intention of the kind." Morand, she insists, is not an "écrivain de combat" (combative writer) (Guitard-Auviste 1981, 135). Finally, Morand himself was fond of protesting that, as far as he was concerned, color was merely a question of aesthetics: "Don't lose sight of the fact that when I take up a subject or work on a story, it is from the point of view of an artist, that is, a man who enjoys the contrast between colors, and who has no desire at all—unlike, for example, an ideologue—to diminish or efface them. Never abandon the aesthetic point of view where I'm concerned. That explains the contradictions and all the rest" (cited in Guitard-Auviste 1981, 135–36).

The question of politics has perhaps been pushed aside so readily because, when Morand's own popularity was at its peak, the political implications of his work were easily submerged in the French obsession with the exotic in the interwar period. It is in the context of the vogue for *la négrophilie* that what might be called the discipline of exoticism, ethnography, became a popular cultural pastime, with its proliferation of societies, expeditions, and museums. Like many of the influential literary works of the period that reflect an ethnographic sensibility (including, notably, works by Leiris, Bataille, and Breton), *Magie noire* was at once a product and an object of this preoccupation with the study of other cultures—as well as a source of dismay for many African-American and Caribbean writers. *Magie noire* had a decidedly cool reception in the United States among African-American intellectuals. J. F. Matthews wrote acerbically that Morand

is of all French writers the one who has contributed the most to the creation of this idea of the American Negro, and to the spread of this idea to the Negro in general. Paul Morand has applied his talent to the study of Negroes in various parts of the globe. What has he concluded? That the Negro, when "civilized," wears his emotions on his sleeve, and is ready to return to the practice of worshiping the gods of the jungle, that he is not far from the pure Negro, and that he is at a level barely more elevated than his ancestors of the Congo and West Africa. (Cited in Guitard-Auviste 1981, 352)

A. James Arnold has noted that Morand provided a "creative irritant" to Negritude writers such as Aimé Césaire, whose *Cahiers d'un retour au pays natal* was inspired in part by one of the *Magie noire* stories (Arnold 1981, 145). Morand capitalized on the ethnographic vogue, using it to cloak his work in an aura of scientific objectivity that, for many, obscured its political dimension. But, as this chapter demonstrates, Morand's objectives ultimately diverge significantly from those of the science he invoked.

ETHNOGRAPHIC AUTHORITY

In his autobiographical preface to *Magie noire*, Morand presents a series of dates followed by brief, documentary-style accounts of seminal moments in his life. This two-page biography does not draw a complete picture of a life but instead mentions only those events that enable readers to account for the fact that Morand, a white man, has written a collection of stories about black people. Events mentioned include sojourns in French colonies and encounters with colonial "others" at circuses, jazz clubs, and military parades. It is the first entry, though, that tells us the most about the author's formation: "1895—Charles, our gardener at Ris-Orangis, shows me the illustrated insert from the *Petit Journal*, which shows a soldier wearing a sugarloaf hat killing Malagasies. Entry of the French in Tananarive" (Morand 1992, 481). This event assumes the status of a primal scene, a moment designated retrospectively as the key to lifelong preoccupations. The oddly Edenesque vignette, depicting an end to innocence wrought by the acquisition of knowledge in a garden (or, in any case, provided by a gardener), marks the author's recognition of his cultural, national, and racial identity and the extent to which this identity is based on the imposition of power. This anecdote serves to bolster the author's ethnographic credentials by establishing a long-standing personal interest in and involvement with the subject, an involvement that, it is suggested, underlies the subsequent knowledge acquired through travel, study, and human experience. To this knowledge, Morand opposes the (black) magic he associates with Africans, a magic of assimilation that obscures essential characteristics, rendering these all but invisible to the untrained eye. Morand implies that this kind of transformation is synonymous with dissimulation. Throughout the *Magie noire* stories, he attempts to combat this transformative "magic" with his own brand of knowledge, by which he will reveal his characters in their natural state, stripped of the mystifying trappings of civilization.

The rest of the *avant-propos* seeks to convince the reader that this knowledge is authoritative. The last four dates in Morand's personal history are followed by a litany of place-names. To cite just one example: "1927.—La Guadeloupe, la Martinique, Trinidad, Curaçao, Haïti, la Jamaïque, Cuba, Alabama, Mississippi" (Morand 1992, 482). Morand provides this list as proof of his ethnographic authority, which he sums up in the final words of the *avant-propos*: "50 000 kilomètres, 28 pays nègres" (482). The author's role here resembles that of a museum curator, collecting cultural artifacts in order to arrange them into meaningful exhibits. Morand was in the habit of depicting himself as an amateur ethnographer; in a passage from his memoir *New York*, set in a Harlem nightclub, he writes, "Suddenly, seeing me note down some impression, one of the habituées approached me and said conspiratorially: '*I see, looking for some material*'" (Morand 1988, 238; emphasized phrase in English in the original). Although Morand is ironizing the pretense of ethnographic authority in this passage, he reclaims this authority when he indicates that he has *translated* the whole exchange from English. By including the nightclub patron's comment in its *version originale*, Morand reasserts not only his difference from the culture he is studying but also the knowledge of the culture that authorizes him to convey that difference to a French audience. He uses the same conceit in his preface to the French edition of Carl Van Vechten's *Nigger Heaven* (titled, in French, *Le Paradis des nègres*), when he introduces readers to a tour guide who will lead them through the wilds of Harlem: "Van Vechten has access to all the souls and all the seedy dives where other Americans wouldn't dare to venture" (Van Vechten 1927, 11). Morand here describes a relationship between observer and observed that is based on a peculiar combination of intimacy and distance (evident in the word "access," which, at the same time that it grants familiarity, reminds readers that it is needed in the first place). Lest there be any misunderstanding about the extraordinary nature of what Van Vechten has accomplished, we are informed that he is "an American of the right shade [*de bon teint*], from old Dutch stock" (Van

Vechten 1927, 11). Morand suggests that Van Vechten possesses a privileged access to knowledge available only to the initiated—in which category Morand appears to include himself.

Morand admired Van Vechten to a large degree because his status as a white American, Morand felt, gave the author of *Nigger Heaven* an especially important vantage point from which to observe Americans of African ancestry. The presence of Africans in the society that, for Morand and for others in the interwar period, was synonymous with modernity, provided the perfect laboratory in which to study the effects of cultural assimilation. Michel Leiris was expressing a widely held view (which he would later come to disavow) when he wrote, in 1930, that African-American culture was the product of two diametrically opposed influences, namely, "on the one hand, a people that could be considered to be still in its infancy when it was transplanted from Africa to America, and on the other hand, a civilization on the cutting edge of capitalist development, the civilization of Fordism and rationalization" (Leiris 1992, 21).[1] Morand was fascinated by what he imagined to be a meeting of extremes in American culture, in which the most primitive of peoples was alienated in the most advanced of societies. Convinced that this rift between a social group and its cultural roots was unnatural, he set himself the task, in the *Magie noire* stories, of identifying those attributes he considered essentially African.

Morand's attempts to capture cultural differences in his texts enact the ethnographic allegory of salvage, a rhetorical strategy that, according to James Clifford, places the ethnographer in the privileged position of "rescuing" a disappearing culture by recording its distinctive features in writing (Clifford 1986, 112). The redemptive nature of salvage ethnography, its claim to preserve the "authentic" or "essential" elements of cultural identity in writing, is based on a pastoral model of prelapsarian harmony, which assumes that corruption and decay have been brought about by increased contact with industrial culture. In his *avant-propos* to *Paris-Tombouctou*, first published in 1928, Morand expressed explicitly his desire to salvage African cultures: "And since, following an implacable law, the steadily increasing flow of white visitors will threaten the original color of these countries, it seemed a good idea to preserve this fleeting moment in which technological miracles enable us to penetrate to the heart of a still-intact nature" (Morand 1981, 7). Morand's view echoed that of the unreconstructed Leiris of 1930: "From the point of view of modern civilization, the Negroes of America are on the road to rapid progress and are tending to lose more and more of their original character" (Leiris 1992, 21). Unlike Leiris, however, who eventually revised his position, Morand clung to these views.

Although ethnography seeks out cultural differences, it does so, according to Clifford, in the service of an underlying common humanity: "Strange behavior is portrayed as meaningful within a common network of symbols—a common ground of understandable activity valid for both observer and observed, and by implication for all human groups. Thus ethnography's narrative of specific differences presupposes, and always refers to, an abstract plane of similarity" (Clifford 1986, 101). The best-known proponent of this position was Lévi-Strauss, who sought above all to reveal, through the almost infinite variety of social structures, the "unshakable basis of human society" (Lévi-Strauss 1977, 445). Morand's motives for appropriating the salvage model, however, differ significantly from those of the ethnographers Clifford discusses. Morand at once appeals to and distorts the salvage model in two of the stories from the *Magie noire* collection set in the United States, "Adieu New York" and "Excelsior."

"Adieu New York!"

In his preface to Van Vechten's book, Morand makes a Lévy-Bruhlian association between Africans and instinct: "Today, instinct tries its luck beneath several banners: but, first and foremost, under the sign of the black flag [*sous pavillon noir*]" (Van Vechten 1927, 11). This image equates Africans with pirates on the attack—a *pavillon noir* is a pirate's flag—and owes its significance to the collapse of its referents: the "noir" refers adjectivally to the flag and metonymically to the people the flag represents (semiotically but not politically). The oscillation thus triggered between the realms of race and representation repeats in microcosm the problematic central to "Adieu New York."

When the story begins, a wealthy American woman named Pamela Freedman is boarding a luxury liner headed to Africa for a pleasure cruise. The promotional poster advertising the cruise leaves no room for doubt about the social status of its clientele: "Refinement. Comfort. Progress. The Mammouth is not an ocean liner, it's a veritable clique, a club limited to two hundred members, the most restricted, the most selective, the most 'exclusive' of clubs" (Morand 1992, 570). This elitist homogeneity is soon threatened by Freedman's presence. The first description of the woman hints that there is something different about her: "Behind the veil that covered her face up to the nose, exotic eyes sparkled" (570–71). From the very beginning, Pamela Freedman's identity is veiled in mystery. After she is mistaken for a servant, a society reporter's inquiry about her origins—"Shall I say you're from New York?" (571)—goes unanswered as the journalist is forced to flee the departing ship. The first section of the story ends with a reference to an "odor of rotten egg" (571) that rises from the depths of the sea, adding a sinister dimension to the woman's failure to disclose her "true" identity and presaging the terrible secret that will eventually surface. When the worst suspicions are finally confirmed by a passenger who recalls having known the woman's mother, "a quadroon named Freeman, like so many other freed slaves" (576)—who, significantly, earned a fortune by inventing a hair-straightening device—an outraged passenger gives voice to the general sentiment: "For a cruise costing ten thousand dollars, it seems to me that we could expect to be among Whites!" (576).

The mysterious woman's presence on the exclusive ship is so incongruous, in fact, that once her "true" identity is discovered, she is literally excluded from it, abandoned at the first port of call in Africa, the victim of a cruel deception. Although distraught at first, Freedman does not remain upset for long; she soon takes up with a colonial official she encounters and fits easily into her role as society hostess for the small community of French colonial administrators. One day, however, she meets Mamadou, an African man to whom she finds herself attracted, who leads—or, more precisely, carries—her to his village: "He wrapped Pamela around his neck as if she were an antelope, and carried her off" (591). "Adieu New York" concludes in a frenzy of racial identification, as the protagonist finally succumbs to the atavistic pull of her ancestral origins, which she has resisted for so long (and whose almost prehistoric nature is suggested by the ship's name, the Mammouth): "She was no longer worth a hundred million dollars; she was worth three oxen, like the other women. She could be seen slapping her hands together, bending over with each beat, feet joined, legs pressed together, rump sticking out, like the negress she had now become" (592).

According to the logic of Morand's story, Freedman could only "now" (*maintenant*) become an African because she always *was* one—beneath the furs and jewels and straightened hair lay an ineffable essence that differentiated her, even if it eluded perception. Little clues are made available to the perceptive reader: there are those exotic eyes mentioned at the beginning of the story, and there's the copy of Gide's *Les Faux monnayeurs* on Freedman's nightstand (573), clues that let us know, if we are open to knowing, that she is a counterfeit. Even a description of the

African foliage evokes her illusory whiteness: "In the electric glow, these grasses appeared white, and everything, even the trunks of the palm trees, was a polar white" (584).

Racial identity for Morand thus proves to be something that both exceeds and precedes one's cultural milieu. This assumption is made manifest when Freedman's masquerade is brought to the attention of the ship's captain because the mysterious woman has neglected to fill in the space marked "race" on the ship's passenger list. The captain's attempt to dismiss the omission as an oversight—"un oubli"—is met with a knowing rebuff: "So, you believe it's possible to forget . . . ? If someone asked you to write down your race, would you forget to say that you're white?" (574). Freedman's silence can only proclaim her guilt, the absence of signs itself significant. Her failure to fill in the blank signals an implicit acknowledgment of the structure of salvage: she knows that to record racial difference would be to realize it, to make it real. What she does not know, however, is that the blanks have been filled in long before her arrival.

The distinctions that salvage authorizes are thematized throughout "Adieu New York," beginning with the protagonist's name, Paméla (in the first edition spelled alternately with and without the *accent aigu*), which gives voice to the caveat "ne *pas mélanger*" (do not mix). Even descriptions of the African jungle seem to warn of the consequences of failing to distinguish adequately among discrete entities: "Everything appeared confused [*confus*], absurd [*absurde*], without form or color. . . . The jumble of roots, the profusion of tangled vines, the riot of parasites appeared inextricable: everything was green. Not a single plain color, a yellow or a white, not a single smooth surface on which to rest the gaze, nothing that wasn't twisted, deformed, tortured [*torturé*], irrational [*irraisonnable*]" (581–82). Such adjectives invest the passage with an emotional force that exceeds the objects being described. This displaced abjection seems better suited to the following passage from a travelogue Morand published in 1929 under the title *Hiver caraïbe*:

> If, in fact, as Emerson said, nature adores mixtures, it does not adore all of them; you can't visit a black college or university in the United States and view these countless hybrids (who are nonetheless dedicated and studious), these European faces trapped beneath hideous woolly hair, these blond or redheaded negresses, these souls tormented by contradictory desires, destroyed in the combat between two heredities, without feeling the anguished pity mixed with repulsion that human abnormalities inspire. (Morand 1929, 51)

It is only by untangling such knots, Morand implies, that the truth can be salvaged.

"Excelsior"

Excelsior is a mythical town in Georgia, where the Bloom family, owners of a funeral home, suffer daily from the stigma attached to their "race." Like the crossroads at which Excelsior "bourgeonne," or blooms (Morand 1992, 544), prefiguring translingually the name of the protagonists, the family's racial identity is situated at the intersection of "blackness" and "whiteness": "There, in an industrial-brick bungalow, . . . lives a white family, or at least a stranger would think so, for, in Excelsior, everyone knows [*chacun sait*] that the Blooms are Blacks. The town records show a 'C' after Victor Bloom's name, which stands for 'color,' as opposed to the 'W' that is the prerogative of white people" (544). Like the *A* that brands Hester Prynne in Hawthorne's *Scarlet Letter*, the letter *C* or *W* tells people what they would not otherwise know but what, once known, becomes part of the lexicon of conventional wisdom contained in the words "chacun sait." The *C* in the Excelsior town register functions like the blank space beside Pamela Freedman's name in "Adieu New York," underwriting an untraceable, unascribable, and therefore inscribable knowledge, whose sourcelessness is the source of its authority.

Only strangers, outsiders, would fail to look beyond the color of the Blooms' skin. Sensing this, the grown Bloom children move to another town, Cornelius Creek, where no one knows their secret, and move quickly up the social ladder. The family is accepted with open arms by Cornelius Creek's upper crust, and one of the siblings, Poolie, wins the favor of the town's most eligible bachelor, who hails from a "famille de vieille souche" (family of old stock) (549). This new life comes to an end, however, the day Poolie's brother Octavius discovers a tiny spot on the back of her neck. The spot gradually grows until it covers all of Poolie's body—and, "what's even more curious, the features themselves seemed to change. The nose lost its pointy solidity, the mouth became more pronounced; an undefinable air of exoticism, which made her all the more radiant, transformed Poolie" (551). Like Pamela Freedman, the Blooms are quickly ostracized from the milieu into which they were so well assimilated: "The Blooms were barred from the country club; they were discouraged from going into the Cornelius Hotel. In church, the minister gave a sermon in which it was said that, at the Last Judgment, the white angels would not associate with the black angels" (554). In the end, the Blooms find happiness and prosperity by accepting their "true" identity: their presence in Cornelius Creek provokes a mass exodus of the town's white residents, enabling the family to buy the surrounding property and build a summer resort for black people. In this paranoid fantasy, the Blooms are depicted implicitly as vultures, profiting from the demise of Cornelius Creek as they profited from the demise of human life while proprietors of the funeral home in Excelsior (the resemblance of this xenophobic nightmare to delusions of Jewish conspiracies is reinforced by the name "Bloom"). As the word "Excelsior" suggests, the family has literally "come up" in the world, the cunning beneficiaries of racial divisiveness.

"Excelsior" ends with an allusion to a southern Creole legend about a "mulatto who wanted to become white but couldn't find the right soap" (555). The legend, when read in conjunction with the opening epigraph attributed to a Dahomean proverb—"A zebra can't change its stripes" (544)—frames the story in words attributed to others. Both the epigraph and the final legend are meant to guide our reading of the story, by referring paradoxically to what it does not say rather than to what it does say. If the proverb is understood to mean that certain traits are essential and therefore resist change, then we could expect to see an illustration of such a trait retaining its essential qualities in the face of change. The change depicted in "Excelsior" is that of a woman whose white skin literally turns black. Even at their most assimilated, the Blooms cannot escape their African ancestry: "The Africans have their fetish days, when they paint their faces different colors; for the Bloom girls, every day at Cornelius Creek was a fetish day, and they were always heavily made up. Their bodies no longer undulated; with their reddish hair straightened, still a bit too stiff and straw-like, they danced the black bottom better than anyone" (550). The transformation the story depicts, then—from white to black—cannot be that evoked in the epigraph, which suggests resistance to change. Nor can it be that found in the closing legend, which tells of a failed attempt to become white. Instead, both proverb and epigraph refer to another transformation—from black to white— that, though not shown in the story, is presupposed. For although Poolie Bloom begins the story with white skin, we are given to understand that white is not her "true," her "original," color. Morand writes that "she had *returned* to being a true mulatto" (553; my emphasis) and puts a similar remark in the mouth of Octavius, who makes the reader's task easier by placing special emphasis on each syllable of the significant word as he tells his sister, "Tu re-tour-nes au noir! [You're tur-ning black again!]" (552). The prefix "re" suggests a return to or a repetition of something that precedes not only the chronology of the narrative but Poolie's own lifetime. But although the one metamorphosis (from white to black) presupposes the other (from black to white), the individual transformation and the generational one are not accorded the same status in the story. Light, Poolie's skin is deceptive, a mask; dark, it is essential, true. It is blackness, not whiteness, that is likened to the indelible stripes of the zebra (which, chromatically speaking, are just as white as they are black). Poolie's metamorphosis, then, is presented as a corrective to the one that history has wrought, a righting of a wrong; the "passing" body lies, and it is the role of the vigilant race-thinker to discover the "truth."[2]

If salvage ethnography converts culture into text, race-thinking takes the conversion a step further by projecting this text onto the human body, which becomes a sign that can be read. In several of the *Magie noire* stories, ideological or other kinds of abstract metamorphoses are accompanied, indeed signaled, by physical transformation: in "Le Tsar noir," for example, Occide's conversion to Communism is illustrated by his adoption of Lenin's goatee, briefcase, and gestures and Trotsky's little steel pince-nez (Morand 1989, 38–39). Paradoxically, however, the more thorough the assimilation, the more visible the subject's "original" identity becomes: Occide's Trotskyite glasses "gave him the appearance of an African fetish" (39). In both "Adieu New York" and "Excelsior," the "passing" body enacts the instability of the signifying system known as "race," an instability that must finally be overridden by the assertion of a certainty that transcends the body. When bodies prove to be illegible, when they fail to signify, when it becomes clear, as Octavius Bloom remarks, that "no one can be sure of his skin!" (Morand 1992, 552), one must turn to signs that have no referent—to a blank in a ship's register or to a *C* that records a color invisible to the naked eye. Morand's bodies lie; but in lying, they tell the truth of their incoherence.

DISAPPEARING ACTS

In his memoir *New York*, Morand wrote of Harlem: "Standing erect at the street crossing symbolic of white civilization, the policeman keeps his eye on this miniature Africa; if that policeman happened to disappear, Harlem would quickly revert to Haiti, given over to voodoo and the rhetorical despotism of a plumed Soulouque" (cited and translated in De Jough 1990, 12). The *Magie noire* stories are filled with disappearing policemen, whose absence ushers in the return of the culturally repressed. When distinctions cannot be drawn synchronically, racist discourse looks to history to make up the difference. The resulting atavism holds assimilation to be impossible, as Morand's stories suggest, because within every "civilized" African—or, in colonial rhetoric, every évolué— there lies a savage struggling to break free.

Morand sought to illustrate this point in a letter to Louis Brun, the publisher of *Magie noire*, in which he described the publicity poster he envisioned for the book: "In the foreground, an American Negro (light coffee-color), red jacket, black ribbon, playing the saxophone; and in the background, the shadow of a black warrior, nude except for a loincloth, a spear, and a long shield. Do this, if possible, with cropped photos" (Morand 1992, 1031). The nude warrior is incarnated as a shadow in the background, never quite distinct but ever present. This image of the savage within presupposes an underlying, essential core that resists change, that remains identical to itself through time. Atavism uses the body as a text, making of it the repository of a prelapsarian identity uncorrupted by modern life. This identity is, of course, also the very difference that prevents Morand's characters from "passing" as white. Its exposure is made possible by salvage, at once a discourse of knowledge production and an investigative fiction that responds to the fear that differences thought to be essential are in danger of disappearing. It is this sense of rapid change—of increasing differentiation from an idealized origin and, thus, of increasing resemblance to the ethnographer's own culture, as we saw in Roussel's *Poussière de soleils*—that prompts the search for the ethnographic image untainted by the proverbial gasoline can or wristwatch, undivided from an originary purity that eludes societies that have been corrupted by modernity.

This concern for preservation prompts the question, What, exactly, is Morand trying to preserve? At first glance, Morand's desire to locate an African purity seems to be coextensive with Lévi-Strauss's classic lamentation of global entropy, in which increasing contact among cultures will end up "working towards the disintegration of the original order of things and hurrying on powerfully organized matter towards ever greater inertia, an inertia which one day will be final" (Lévi-Strauss 1977, 472). Lévi-Strauss's concern about encroaching inertia, or lack of differentiation, is echoed in Morand's condemnation of increasing cultural homogenization in *Hiver caraïbe*: "Black is beautiful, just as white is beautiful; it's gray that is ugly" (Morand 1929, 83). But unlike Lévi-Strauss, for whom cultural differences serve to reinforce "the brotherhood of man" (448), Morand does not attempt to reinscribe difference into an ethnographic vision of the world linked by a common humanity. Instead, he invokes difference as both a means and an end.

It is in his statements about immigration that Morand's priorities are perhaps the clearest, revealing the ethnic hierarchies that underlie his prescriptions for cultural separatism. In *Hiver caraïbe*, he writes, "Let's create, regardless of cost, a strong monitoring of foreigners within our borders, to replace those wretched gendarmes, who are incapable of distinguishing between an Eskimo and an Arab" (Morand 1929, 248). Morand calls this proposal a measure of "self-defence" (Morand 1929, 248; the English expression, with the British spelling, is Morand's), using a foreign expression to justify the exclusion of foreignness. His admiration for Gobineau, whose *Essai sur l'inégalité des races humaines* he carried in his suitcase as he collected "field notes" for *Hiver caraïbe*, is apparent in his prescription for an "Aryan" France: "In a hundred years, what will our blood be? We need Celtic blood, Saxon and Germanic blood, Nordic blood. Instead, we have Levantines, Semites, Berbers, and Southern Latins entering our country, races of traffickers and future politicians" (Morand 1929, 248–49). Similarly, in *Paris-Tombouctou*, Morand expresses his fear that increasing contact with "southern" cultures will result in the dilution of "northern" blood: "The North debases itself each time it mixes with the Midi. The rush to the Côte d'Azur is a prologue to the Negro craze" (1981, 50). The hierarchy invoked in these statements is unmistakable, taking us far from humanistic anthropological ideals and closer to the fear, which Morand voices in the 1926 travel account *Rien que la terre*, that the white race will succumb to the invasion of "Chinois et Nègres" (1993, 31).

What has confused many scholars, however, is the fact that not only is Morand eager to salvage distinctions among races; he is also anxious to distinguish among racisms, using the same pretense of impartiality to differentiate his own racism from that of others. In the *Magie noire* stories, "bad" American racism is compared unfavorably with "good" French racism. The use of free indirect discourse in "Excelsior," for example, encourages readers to sympathize with the Blooms' plight: "Outside America, outside the South, outside Excelsior, no one would have dreamed of considering the Blooms black . . . so, why always make distinctions?" (1992, 547). In the face of their oppression, the Blooms' anxiety is shown to be eminently justified, their objections entirely rational: "The only time anyone let me go ahead of them," said Octavius, "was in battle" (546). The reader cannot fail to become indignant at the injustice of American racism. Similarly, the prejudice of the ship's passengers who shun Pamela Freedman in "Adieu New York" is depicted as petty and illogical, especially when pointed out by the one passenger—named Nathan Jonas—whose own marginal status as a member of another persecuted group, Jews, enables him to grasp the irony of the situation (although it is his eagerness to deflect his own difference onto her that results in the woman's abandonment): "Let's see now . . . ; you lay out ten thousand dollars to go see some Negroes, you get to see some before the scheduled date, and you're not happy, ladies?" (576).[3] Morand's critique of American racism as cruel and arbitrary serves to make his own seem good-natured, an unpleasant and reluctant necessity. The differentiation that invariably overtakes the *Magie noire* stories thus occurs as if against the narrator's wishes, providing a decidedly unrhetorical answer to the Blooms' seemingly rhetorical question, "Pourquoi différer toujours?" (Why always make distinctions?). In the description of the African man who ultimately wins Pamela Freedman over in "Adieu New York," the narrative's distancing from one form of racism legitimates another, which, despite its outlandishness, is presented as a moderate alternative to the American variety: "No, the sight of a white woman did not make him crazy, as the lynchers of Virginia claim; he took Paméla as he would any other woman; he had for women the enormous and indiscriminate appetite of the black male, to whom only quantity matters" (593).

This distinction between forms of racism, however, is undermined in another story from the *Magie noire* collection which is also set partly in the United States and which seems to suggest a certain affinity between Morand's objectives and those of the "lyncheurs de Virginie." In "Syracuse ou l'homme-panthère," a thoroughly assimilated African-American media mogul named Lincoln Vamp is constantly urging other African-Americans to "forget Africa." While in Belgium attending a conference, Vamp visits the Belgian Congo museum, where an exhibit of ceremonial burial artifacts causes him to hallucinate:

> These African beliefs that make of the ritual clothes of the deceased so many extensions of his living person awoke in the heart of the citizen from Syracuse; all the diviners, the necromants who had slipped on these accursed, cast-off garments, all the souls that had been trapped in these calabashes, all the lifeless locks of hair that had been slipped into magic pouches came back to life, signaled their presence. "Flee," they said; "leave the land that you inhabit; it is fertile only in appearance, but ruin is upon it. Its progress is nothing but prestige; it has made of you a vampire. Return to the land where the trees and the stones speak in the name of the Spirit." (Morand 1992, 566)

The spirits that haunt Lincoln Vamp point out to him the error of his ways; instead of "forgetting Africa," as he has tried so hard to do, he is urged, if only by his own conscience, to shed the ephemeral trappings of the New

World and embrace the timeless truths of the Old. It is no accident that Vamp's name evokes "vampire," an image that was sometimes used to refer to the absorption or cannibalization of another culture, such as in Robert Aron and Arnaud Dandieu's 1931 tract *Le Cancer américain*, which termed "vampirisme" America's influence on Europe. In "Charleston," another story in the *Magie noire* collection, a white character speaks of Africans' "love of real blood" (Morand 1992, 96). Morand's vampire imagery also recalls the biochemical index of blood types that, as we have seen, was invoked in the interwar years by proponents of cultural separatism.

Implicit in this affirmation of the glories of Africa is the suggestion, echoed in "Adieu New York," that people of African descent *belong* in Africa (or at the very least, sequestered in communities with others like them, as in "Excelsior"). This suggestion carries with it very practical and very grave implications concerning immigration. From the ostensibly innocuous thesis that modern life corrupts to the assertion that immigration should be restricted, the distance is not very great: in *Hiver caraïbe*, Morand concludes that "a border should be able to open and close like a drain" (249). These words were written in 1929, just two years before the French government reversed its comparatively liberal policy of the preceding decades, drastically curtailing immigration and expatriating many of the immigrants already in France. (From 1921 to 1931, the immigrant population rose from 1.5 million to roughly 2.9 million, whereas between 1931 and 1936, it decreased to 2.4 million.)[4]

It is in this context that we must hear the voices urging Lincoln Vamp to "leave the land that he inhabits." But we must be attuned as well to the language of Morand's story, in which the word used for land, "terre," also means earth; in the context of the burial artifacts that provoke the hallucination, the passage might be understood to suggest that Vamp would be better off leaving this earth altogether. The two readings of this passage (implications about immigration on the one hand and about death on the other) are not contradictory but in fact reinforce one another. In the modern era, displacement and death have often gone together, from colonial "pacification" campaigns to the Vichy government's active involvement in the deportation of French Jews and non-Jewish foreign nationals during World War II. Ultimately, the key to the work of Paul Morand can be found in the primal scene he so carefully lays out for us in the preface to *Magie noire*, in the image of the slaughtered Malagasy soldiers, which shows that the fetishization of alterity ultimately serves to eliminate it.

Epilogue

Black-Blanc-Beur

Late in the evening of July 12, 1998, 1.5 million people crowded onto the Champs-Élysées as the enormous neon face of Zinedine Zidane beamed down from above, projected against the Arc de Triomphe; from all corners of the capital, car horns could be heard honking into the early hours. France had just won the World Cup, against all odds and all expectation, and suddenly the nation, which until very recently had been largely indifferent to the sport, was transformed into a giant soccer stadium.

In the media, the victory, which boosted Jacques Chirac's standing in the opinion polls (*Le Monde*, July 28, 1998, 5), was widely interpreted as a triumph of "l'intégration." The historian Georges Vigarello's remarks in a special postgame issue (no. 1758, July 18) of *Le Nouvel observateur* (henceforth *N.O.*) were typical of the rhetoric used in the heady days and weeks following the final match: "The players, flag-bearers of a multicultural France, have done more for integration than ten or fifteen years of voluntarism" (37). Yet only four weeks earlier the French team had been dismissed on the basis of its ethnic makeup. As Gérard Ejnès, writing in *L'Équipe*, the sports paper, complained, "This isn't a football team; it's a corner grocery" (35). Ejnès was alluding to the number of corner grocery shops in urban centers owned by North Africans. With France's unanticipated sporting victory, however, the diversity that had previously been seen as a liability suddenly became a great asset: "Tonight, the three colors of France are black, white, and brown" ["black, blanc, beur"—the third term being a slang word for North African] (22). The team's success was immediately transfigured into a metaphor for national unity, with implications that extended far beyond the soccer field.

In many ways, the rhetoric used to celebrate the victory recalled that used in constructing the notion of *la plus grande France*: "To these four World Cups, France was able to oppose its five continents" (Martin-Casteneau, *Libération*, July 18–19, 1998). The suggestion of possession apparent in the use of the possessive adjective "ses" (its) evokes an unreconstructed sense of colonial propriety, as if decolonization had been nothing but a bad dream. The evocation of France's colonial past exemplifies one of what Kristin Ross has called "the various ways in which the practice of colonialism outlived its history" (Ross 1996, 7). Ross is referring to the period immediately following decolonization, but the parapraxes of the colonial unconscious are still in evidence at the end of the twentieth century. The expression "black-blanc-beur," echoing the colors of the French flag (*bleu-blanc-rouge*), was invoked constantly, in virtually every publication that carried news of the victory, and often as a caption beneath photos of a white player flanked by a black player and a North African player. Both the image and the accompanying rhetoric bear a remarkable resemblance to a well-known 1941 poster by Eric Castel whose caption reads: "Trois couleurs, un drapeau, un empire" (Three colors, one flag, one empire).

But the colonial empire was more than an iconographic presence in the weeks following the World Cup; it was often invoked explicitly, as in this piece of human-interest reportage: "9:00 P.M. local time in Petit Canal: The Indian community celebrates the French victory. The children have the *tricolore* painted on their faces. 'Like all minorities from the former French empire, we side with the *métropole*,' says a doctor whose family is originally from Mahé" (Olivier Péretié et al., *N.O.* 1758, 27). The travelogue style of this piece recalls Paul Morand's whirlwind tour of the colonies in his preface to *Magie noire*; here tattoos and warpaint have been replaced by the *tricolore*. With the desire to preserve *la plus grande France* conveniently articulated by a "minority," metropolitan French readers may be reassured of the undying loyalty of France's (post)colonial subjects. The borders of the *hexagone* have been redrawn, however. The coordinates of imperial geography designate Marseille a colonial outpost whose inhabitants are permitted a brief and charmingly carniva-

Figure 15. *Poster by Eric Castel: "Three colors, one flag, one empire." Courtesy Musée d'histoire contemporaine, Paris.*

lesque reversal of center and periphery: "The residents of Marseille transform Canebière and Vieux-Port into the center of the universe for a night, as in the colonial period.... African matrons [*des mamans africaines*] beat the tom-tom. As for the rest, it is difficult to determine the color of people's skin beneath the red, white, and blue face paint" (*N.O.* 1758, 30). Marseille can become the center of the universe only by means of an inversion that first entails being pushed outside the boundaries of what Herman Lebovics calls "True France," before being brought back as a resident alien, a stranger within. All eyes are on Marseille, as all gazes were fixed on the *cités indigènes* at the colonial exhibitions. The city becomes a living museum, a permanent exhibt, as its soccer fans are transformed into tribal objects of anthropological study by sociologist Jean Viard: "In this city, soccer has always served as a totem uniting an entire people" (31).

But why, after all, go to Marseille, let alone Guadeloupe, when the delights of the empire can be sampled simply by taking a stroll around the Stade de France, newly accessible by métro (as was the Bois de Vincennes in 1931)? "On the playing field, the French team presents two intersecting journeys, a fabulous voyage around the globe and a promenade through the highways and byways of the French countryside. The itinerary begins in the Loyauté Islands . . . " (32). Rhetoric such as this placed Paris at the center of a resuscitated colonial empire raised from the ashes of the wars of independence. France's phantasmatic colonial possessions were so many provincial regions at the periphery, all succumbing to the unifying force of the center. The whole world ("the globe," "the five continents") was gathered on the playing field in Saint-Denis—and the whole world was French, from "les îles Loyauté" to "la Nouvelle-Calédonie" to Point-à-Pître, birthplace of the star player of the semifinal game, Lilian Thuram, whose "heart wavers between childhood games on the beach and Fontainebleau, where his mother, six kids in tow, had come to seek a salary" (32). Thuram's divided loyalty is not unlike that of Zouzou, torn between Haiti and her gilded cage in Paris, or Zizou, nickname of star player Zinedine Zidane, "that shy kid born to Kabyle parents in a housing project in the northern part of Marseille," and who, therefore, "knows the value of this bit of blue cloth that is the French players' uniform" (32). Just as the *tirailleurs sénégalais* were routinely depicted eagerly donning military uniforms and fighting patriotically for France, the players on the French team with colonial backgrounds were repeatedly shown to be grateful for the chance to do battle for the mother country against a common enemy.

Surprisingly, however, France's real rivals were not Italy or Brazil, its opponents in the final and semifinal, respectively. As in the interwar period, the French opposed their sense of national unity during the World Cup to that of their closest international competitors, Germany and Britain: "The melting pot, certainly, exists, unlike the German situation, where there are no Turkish players on the national football team, and unlike the English team, too, where players from the former Commonwealth are rare" (37). This comparison of the ethnic makeup of competing football teams reveals more than sporting strategy. It implies a comparison of different perceptions of national identity, perceptions that are invoked not only as discourses *about* identity but also as expressions *of* identity.

Since the appearance of Ernest Renan's "Qu'est-ce qu'une nation?" at the end of the nineteenth century, it has become a commonplace of political theory to reiterate the distinction between the contractual model of community, associated with France, and that associated with Germany (Renan 1947–61, 887–906). Julia Kristeva, for example, adopting this model unproblematically, writes: "Quite the opposite of the 'spirit of the people' (*Volksgeist*), whose origins have been traced back to the ambiguities of the great Herder and that is mystically rooted in the soil, the blood, and the genius of the language, the French Enlightenment is embodied in the French Republic, is achieved in a legal and political pact between free and equal individuals" (Kristeva 1993, 39–40). Rogers Brubaker, too, opposes what he terms France's "concentric" and "assimilationist" conception of nationhood to a "bounded," "differentialist," and "ethnocultural" ideal based on essentialist notions of group identity—which he attributes to Germany (Brubaker 1992, 5, 6, and passim). Brubaker acknowledges that both discourses have at certain moments coexisted in France (during the Dreyfus affair, the interwar period, the Vichy regime, and again in recent years), when "the prevailing French idiom of nationhood—state-centered and assimilationist—has been challenged by a more ethnocultural counteridiom" (13–14). But by presenting these historical moments as anomalous blips in an otherwise uniform national landscape, these authors are creating a simplistic binary between ethnocultural and assimilationist conceptions of nationhood. Paul Morand's racial fantasies were not a "counteridiom" any more than the *Front national* is; both phenomena are an integral part of the French cultural idiom itself. To relegate exclusionary discourses in France to the status of a "challenge" posed to a "dominant" assimilationist discourse is to overlook the fact that these have always coexisted in what Maxim Silverman calls "a single anthropological project in the modern era" (Silverman 1992, 25).

In the summer of 1998, commentators implicitly invoked Renan, as they had between the wars, in distinguishing the French concept of nationhood from that of Germany. Not only, it was suggested, do France and Germany define nationhood in different ways; these different definitions also define the nations themselves. France, in other words, differs from Germany precisely to the extent that it defines nationhood differently: "Law of the soil and not of blood, the absolute primacy of that which unites over that which separates, the relegation of particularities to the private sphere, the definition of the nation as adherence to a common destiny, and as working toward the universal: these are the characteristics of the open but firm conception that is opposed to the 'differentialisms' practiced by our neighbors" (François Dufay, *Le Point* 1348, July 18, 1998, 29). By 1998, however, the terms of Renan's distinction had been altered: the soil had replaced the social contract, suggesting that immigration had been factored into the equation of national unity and that a mythical "destiny" had replaced the mythical origin in the national consciousness.

This common destiny is the postcolonial version of a common origin, in which "nos ancêtres les Gaulois" (our forefathers the Gauls) is replaced by "nos enfants les bleus" (our soccer team, children of France). This destiny, like the mythical origin it replaces, is bound up in the notion of a national character, the identification of a difference that could unite the French at the same time that it distinguished them from everyone else. In response to the question whether the French feared losing their national identity in the face of increasing European unification and global competition, Philippe Séguin replied with a question: "Let's get this straight: would we like the Scots as much without their kilts, their whisky flasks and their chants, or the Brazilians without their samba and their carefree nature? What a dull world it would be if we all resembled each other! The beauty in the stadiums came from the different spots of color" (28). Séguin's message is indeed clear: each nation should unite around a common costume (the Scots' kilt, France's blue soccer uniform), a common character trait (the Brazilians' "insouciance")—in short, a common stereotype. Yet Séguin confuses the loss of national identity with the loss of individual identity. In seeking to preserve international distinctions (whisky, the samba), he is imposing national homogeneity. The "different spots of color" that he wishes to see can only be the collective colors of uniforms. The "black-blanc-beur" image of national unity is not an old model of integration but, rather, a new model of empire.

As Alain de Benoist, spokesman for the New Right in France, explains: "The principle of empire tries to reconcile the one and the many, the particular and the universal" (Benoist 1993–94, 88). Benoist opposes empire to nation on the basis of its emphasis on group identities: "The empire requires the preservation of the diversity of groups; by its very logic, the nation recognizes only individuals" (90). Although it is true that the French nation officially recognizes only individuals, and not subgroups within the national community (as the *affaire du foulard*, in which Muslim girls were forbidden to wear headscarves that would signal their membership in a particular religious group, demonstrated), unconsciously, imperial rhetoric infuses the language of cultural difference. But the French colonial model of empire, which, as we have seen, is still invoked proudly, poses a problem for Benoist's model of imperial culture. *La plus grande France*, Benoist argues, was not an empire in the true sense: "Such a designation is only abusively given to enterprises or powers merely engaged in expanding their national territory" (93). It is here that we witness the return of the colonial unconscious. In his discussion of the political formations for which he rejects the term "empire," such as "the Napoleonic empire, Hitler's Third Reich, the French and British colonial empires, and modern imperialisms of the American and Soviet types" (93), Benoist treats each of these "pseudoempires" in turn, *with the exception of colonialism*, which he neglects to take up again. This is because France's colonial history renders obsolete the distinction, in the French context, between nation and empire. The overlooked but persistently present element in discussions of French national identity today, the differentialist discourse of France's colonial legacy, creates an empire within the nation, a national empire, in relation to which former colonial subjects and their families are the "foreigners within."

The insistence on diversity in the heady days following France's victory in the World Cup was so great that the objects of the discourse of difference were sometimes designated its subjects, the *sujets de l'énoncé* transformed into *sujets de l'énonciation*. As Claude Imbert wrote in his editorial in *Le Point* in the week following the final match, "People are right to admire successful integration within a team of Kabyles, Africans, Armenians, etc. In truth, the so-called racism of the French is rarely directed at immigrants who are integrated. Instead, it is aroused by those who refuse our morals and our laws by entrenching themselves in their differences" (*Le Point* 1348, July 18, 1998, 5). It is "they" who impose difference, while "we" talk only of its abolition in assimilation, in integration. "We" reluctantly go along with these differences—and secretly cling to the divisions they entail. The celebration of difference is seen as a definitive departure from racism (here as in the work of Paul Morand). But as Pierre-André Taguieff points out, "The norm of respect for difference, far from embodying that fundamental human right which is the right of difference, serves to make presentable, even honorable, the obsession with contact—the phobia of mixing—which is the core of racism" (Taguieff 1993–94, 123).

The World Cup victory brought out this obsession with contact even as it celebrated team spirit. As I hope to have shown, the origins of what Ross calls "the neoracist consensus of today" (1996, 196) can be traced back to the period between the wars when, time after time, cultural texts showed that the desire to preserve cultural distance—the essence of the colonial unconscious—underlay expressions of exoticism that seemed to promote contact between cultures. A discourse of exposure at the colonial exhibitions actually concealed an aesthetic, and an ethic, of separatism reinforced by pseudoscientific theories of racial identity. The figure of the hybrid, exhibited both at the Miss France d'Outre-Mer contest and in Raymond Roussel's play *L'Etoile au front*, reinforced the very divisions it appeared to eradicate. Similarly, discourses of discovery and atavistic constructions of the primitive were grounded in a temporal alterity (*La Poussière de soleils, Magie noire*), while digestive models of assimilation (*Babylone, Princesse Tam-Tam*) were shown to lead to disastrous results (cannibalism, the fall of the Roman empire). And those colonials who might manage to accede to the higher echelons of French cultural life were apparently doomed to an existence of unhappy isolation (*Zouzou*).

All the cultural texts studied here harbor what Taguieff calls a "differentialist racism" (1993–94, 101), concealed within their celebration of cultural diversity. By juxtaposing the colonial exhibitions—official, state-sponsored events—with more subtle expressions of colonial ideology in individual works of art, I have sought to demonstrate the ubiquity of certain assumptions about identity and difference in interwar France. Rather than consider these assumptions to be diluted because they appeared at all levels of cultural production (popular and avant-garde literature, theater, film, and world's fairs), we must interpret the fact that they were taken for granted—not given a second thought—as a sign of their insidious force. This quiet but powerful influence is a function of what, after Arendt, we might call the banality of colonial culture, its seeming ordinariness and unquestioned pervasiveness in everyday life.

Despite the fact that these assumptions were everywhere in circulation, they were nonetheless hidden from view. Colonial culture's manifest content, the discourse of assimilation, concealed a latent but powerful desire for cultural separatism. These apparently incompatible visions of French identity were complementary—indeed, often inseparable—but they have rarely been seen as such. The Enlightenment concept of universalism was never invoked more emphatically than in the colonial discourse of the Third Republic; yet, even in the frenzied heyday of French colonial rhetoric in the period between the world wars, the prospect of cultural assimilation was constantly overshadowed by the combined fear of and insistence on cultural difference. The importance of the colonial project in constructing French cultural and national identity cannot be overemphasized: it was by looking to the outside world that France was able to create and zealously guard the myth of a nation of insiders, causing the "inside" to recede endlessly beyond the grasp of many of its inhabitants. The colonial unconscious is the site of intersection between imperialism and nationalism, a site on which identity and difference could—and can—both exist, not in confrontation or contradiction but as complementary expressions of a single conception of nationhood.

Notes

1. Unless otherwise noted, all translations are my own.
2. See Lebovics 1994 and Norindr 1996 for discussions of the Exposition coloniale.
3. For a history of the policies of assimilation and association, see Betts 1961.
4. For further discussion of the assimilation myth in colonial (and postcolonial) discourse, see Andrew and Kanya-Forstner 1981, 243–45 and passim, and Silverman 1992, 31, 95–125.
5. Of assimilation, Lewis (1962) writes: "What was wrong with 'assimilation' was not that it was illogical, unrealistic, or impossible, but rather that no serious effort was ever made to carry it out" (153); association he characterizes as a retreat from the pretense of democracy, an attempt "to reassure Frenchmen that they were not about to be inundated by the votes of millions of natives in the French colonies" (151).
6. Henry Louis Gates, Jr., for example, contends that "race . . . pretends to be an objective term of classification, when in fact it is a dangerous trope" (1986, 5).

1. Colonialism Exposed

1. For a detailed account of the ECI, see Lebovics 1994, chap. 2.
2. The Procès-Verbal of October 12, 1935, specifies that "each possession or colony will subsidize the lodging of the natives brought over to participate in [*figurer à*] the exhibition *in the same buildings in which they will work*" (Archives Nationales [henceforth A.N.] F12 12384, file 1; original emphasis).
3. For accounts of undercover surveillance of Indochinese participants in the 1931 exhibition as well as of other Indochinese in Paris, see the files stamped "SE-CRETS," mostly originating from the Service de Contrôle et d'Assistance en France des indigènes des colonies françaises, in A.N. (Aix-en-Provence) slot-

fom III/5. See also Lebovics's discussion of this underground activity in *True France*.

4. On the "ville-usine" in France, see Gaudemar 1982, 44–49.
5. On the Jardin d'Acclimatation and the use of "human showcases" in international exhibitions, see Greenhalgh 1988, 82–111. On the participation of colonial subjects in world's fairs of the nineteenth century, see Marie-Noëlle Pradel-de Grandy, "Découverte des civilisations dans l'espace et dans le temps," in *Le Livre des expositions universelles, 1851–1989* (1983).
6. According to Lois W. Banner (1984, 255), the first modern beauty contest was held in New York in 1854, the brainchild of P. T. Barnum.
7. Citing David Lloyd George, Hannah Arendt writes that "Clemenceau insisted at the peace table in 1918 that he cared about nothing but 'an unlimited right of levying black troops to assist in the defense of French territory in Europe if France were attacked in the future by Germany' " (Arendt 1968, 9).
8. Schneider also cites a 1938 pamphlet written by Jean-Marie Baron that calls type-B blood "the source of all social ills" (1990b, 254).
9. In *Black Skin, White Masks*, Franz Fanon writes of the imbalance of power that cuts across personal and political lines: "Since he is the master and more simply the male, the white man can allow himself the luxury of sleeping with many women. This is true in every country and especially in the colonies. But when a white woman accepts a black man there is automatically a romantic aspect. It is a giving, not a seizing" (1967, 46n).
10. Since Mulvey's article first appeared in 1975, much has been written to problematize it. See, for example, Stacey 1992, 244–47; Rodowick 1982, 4–15; and Mulvey 1989, 29–39. It is not within the scope of this book to comment on the adequacy or implications of Mulvey's arguments for the discipline of film theory.

2. RAYMOND ROUSSEL AND THE STRUCTURE OF STEREOTYPE

1. Roussel himself promoted the comparison with *Hernani* by commissioning a painting that depicted, on one half of the canvas, the "bataille d'*Hernani*" and, on the other half, a performance of *Étoile* (Ferry 1953, 160–61).
2. Roussel was not unfamiliar with the concept of the unconscious, having undergone psychoanalytic treatment with Pierre Janet, who wrote a case study of Roussel using the pseudonym "Martial," after the protagonist of *Locus Solus*. Roussel proudly reproduced the study in *Comment j'ai écrit certains de mes livres*, apparently grateful for any form of recognition whatsoever, even at the expense of being called "un pauvre petit malade."
3. One comeback is recounted by Roussel himself in *Comment*, with characteristic self-congratulation: "During the second act, after one of my adversaries had yelled to those who were applauding, 'Professional claque!' Robert Desnos retorted: 'If we're the claque, you're the cheek [*la joue*].' This reply met with success and was quoted by many newspapers. (It is amusing to note that by inverting the 'l' and the 'j' [in 'la joue'], one ends up with 'We're the claque

and you're jealous [*jaloux*],' a phrase that would not have been inaccurate)" (32).

4. Sjef Houppermans relates an anecdote that illustrates Roussel's obsession with the notion of minimal difference: "After seeing the same play dozens of times at the theater, Roussel exclaimed to a friend: ' . . . you can't imagine how fascinating it is to observe the tiniest differences in the way the actors play their roles' " (Houppermans 1985, 157).

5. Patrick Gregory, the translator of the English-language edition of *La Violence et le sacré*, corrects Girard's mistake in his translation of Girard's translation: "A crowd of people" (212). The English translation of *Totem and Taboo* from the *Standard Edition* that Gregory cites earlier gives "a company of individuals" (Girard 1977, 202).

6. Jean Ferry has summarized the labyrinthine chain of clues in the "appendice à l'appendice" to *Une étude sur Raymond Roussel* (1953, 163–76).

7. Roussel was fond of this conceit. Many of his works contain episodes in which something is hidden in such a way that it can be found only by a certain person after a carefully calculated effort. In *L'Étoile au front*, one anecdote tells of a nun marking a statue with a symbol visible only from a certain angle in the moonlight, so that it will be recognized by her former lover but will remain imperceptible to everyone else (Roussel 1963a, 23–30). Other variations on this theme can be found in *Locus Solus* (1965, 16–29 and 195–215).

8. This image recalls a similar (and greatly detailed) description in *La Seine* of a ray of sunlight illuminating floating dust particles (Roussel 1994, 353–55).

9. There is another variation on the theme of excised sections of famous literary works, involving a manuscript of the "lost fifth act" of Shakespeare's *Romeo and Juliet*, in *Impressions d'Afrique* (Roussel 1963b, 107–13, 212–14, and 216–18).

10. The best-known proponent of this position was Lucien Lévy-Bruhl (1960).

3. Cannibals in Babylon

1. For the most comprehensive bibliography of Crevel's work and Crevel scholarship, see Rochester 1978, 135–73.

2. See Lévi-Strauss 1979a, 505. For a study of the role of silverware in the history of civilization, see Elias 1978, 84–129 and 122–29.

3. Hannah Arendt attributes the essay's belated popularity to the atmosphere of pessimism and the perception of decadence that surrounded the First World War, noting that "doctrines of decay seem to have some very intimate connection with race-thinking" (1968, 51).

4. See Crevel 1929, chap. 3, for an account of the author's experience on the psychoanalyst's couch.

5. Crevel alludes to *Totem and Taboo*, published in French translation in 1924, in a 1933 essay called "Notes en vue d'une psycho-dialectique." This essay, which includes a critique of the recently published thesis of a young doctor named Jacques Lacan (whom Crevel presciently suggests will be Freud's successor),

condemns psychoanalysis for being either too materialist—as in Freud's more biologistic moments—or not materialist enough, as when psychoanalysts neglect the role of social and economic factors in their patients' lives. After deriding the "matérialisme mécanique" of Freud's suggestion that operating on a patient's testicles will "cure" him of his homosexuality, Crevel adds, "However, from the psychoanalytic point of view, the close study of the testicles and the psycho-clinical examination of the affected person might have taught us more than all the abstract hypotheses advanced in connection with the totemic meal" (1986, 288–89).

6. Reprinted in Crevel 1974, 182–84.

7. Michel Carassou notes that Crevel had originally planned to call the novel *La Femme et la ville* (1989, 119). Crevel pursues this association in a metaphor that extends throughout the first chapter of *Êtes-vous fous?*, which begins with the image of a feminized city: "The City. She wears a necklace of papier mâché faces, but her headdress playfully resembles the Arc de Triomphe" (Crevel 1929, 10).

4. A Colonial Princess

1. Andrew writes: "The bal stands opposite the music-hall in every respect. It rejects illusion, technology, grandeur and passive spectacle in favor of modesty and participation (the clients dance, talk and even sing). Moreover, like the café-concert of the nineteenth century, it fostered a family atmosphere" (1992, 27).

2. These expressions of ambivalence toward sound are all the more remarkable given that Marc Allégret, along with André Gide and others associated with the *Nouvelle Revue Française* (e.g., Giraudoux, Martin du Gard, Maurois, Morand, and Romains), had tried to form a production company called the Film Parlant Français. See Durosay 1993, 194–97.

3. The film's underlying emphasis on difference was echoed by contemporary reviewers, who were not indifferent to Baker's "race." In the last days of 1934, Lucienne Escoube wrote, "Zouzou, the lovely Zouzou, sings, dances, goes about her business with the devilish rhythm that is a trademark of the black race, a sort of explosive and infectious job, an innate music that explains the kind of fascination that such a creature holds for tired whites, most of whom have not experienced joy firsthand" (*Pour Vous*, Dec. 27, 1934, no. 319, p. 7). The reviewer goes on to speak of "the famous dynamism of her race."

5. Difference in Disguise

1. Leiris's disclaimer can be found in a note in the same volume: "Of course, this ancient text no longer reflects the view that the author now has of 'Negritude' " (Leiris 1992, 265–66).

2. In *Papiers d'identitié*, Morand described the transformation of his own appearance—only Morand viewed his own supposed metamorphosis as a "deforma-

tion" rather than, as in the case of Poolie Bloom, an atavistic "return." After viewing a portrait of him drawn by Jean Cocteau in 1928, shortly after the publication of *Magie noire*, he wrote: "Not only is our moral persona deformed by fame, but so are our physical features. Each of the features of which I am composed today after ten years of literary life has been shaped by one of my books . . . and after *Magie noire*, even photos of me have begun, in the manner of Dorian Gray, to acquire Negroid characteristics!" (cited in Collomb 1993, 22–23).

3. For a particularly virulent example of Morand's antisemitism, see his *France-la-doulce* (Paris: Gallimard, 1934), a satire meant to show the extent to which the French film industry had been taken over by Jews and immigrants.

4. A similar sense of menace is apparent several decades later, in the context of decolonization. In his preface to the 1967 edition of Blaise Cendrars's *Du monde entier*, Morand wrote of the "threat" posed then by "the birth of an Africa much more ominous [*ténébreuse*] than Conrad's Africa" (Cendrars 1993, 11).

Bibliography

Abel, Richard. 1988. *French Film Theory and Criticism, 1907–1939*. Vol. 2. Princeton: Princeton University Press.

Adams, Mark B., ed. 1990. *The Wellborn Science*. New York: Oxford University Press.

Aldrich, Robert. 1996. *Greater France: A History of Overseas Expansion*. London: Macmillan.

Anderson, Benedict. 1993. *Imagined Communities: Reflections on the Origin and Spread of Nationalism*. Rev. ed. London: Verso.

Andrew, Christopher M., and A. S. Kanya-Forstner. 1981. *France Overseas: The Great War and the Climax of French Imperial Expansion*. London: Thames & Hudson.

Andrew, Dudley. 1992. "Family Diversions: French Popular Cinema and the Music-Hall." In *Popular European Cinema*, ed. Richard Dyer and Ginette Vincendeau, 15–30.London: Routledge.

——. 1995. *Mists of Regret: Culture and Sensibility in Classic French Film*. Princeton: Princeton University Press.

Angoulvant, G. 1931. "L'Afrique Occidentale Française." *Revue des Deux Mondes* 4 (July): 834–54.

Arendt, Hannah. 1968. *Imperialism*. San Diego: Harcourt Brace Jovanovich.

Arens, W. 1979. *The Man-Eating Myth: Anthropology and Anthropophagy*. New York: Oxford University Press.

Aristotle. 1987. *Poetics*. Trans. Richard Janko. Indianapolis: Hackett.

Arnold, A. James. 1981. *Modernism and Negritude*. Cambridge: Harvard University Press.

Aron, Robert, and Arnaud Dandieu. 1931. *Le Cancer américain*. Paris: Rieder.

Artaud, Adrian. 1924. *Exposition nationale coloniale de Marseille: Rapport général*. Marseille: Commissariat général.

Augé, Marc. 1972. "Les Métamorphoses du vampire." *Nouvelle Revue de Psychanalyse* 6 (Fall): 129–46.

Baker, Jean-Claude, and Chris Chase. 1993. *Josephine: The Hungry Heart*. New York: Random House.

Balandier, Georges. 1984. "Préface." *Histoire* 69.

Balibar, Etienne. 1984. "Sujets ou citoyens." *Les Temps modernes,* nos. 452–54: 1726–53.

Banner, Lois W. 1984. *American Beauty*. Chicago: University of Chicago Press.

Barthes, Roland. 1957. *Mythologies*. Paris: Seuil.

——. 1987. *Mythologies*. Trans. Annette Lavers. New York: Hill and Wang.

Bataille, Georges. 1967. *La Part maudite*. Paris: Minuit.

Beauregard, Victor. 1924. *L'Empire colonial de la France: Formation, résultats, destinées*. Paris: Société d'éditions géographiques, maritimes et coloniales.

Bell, Susan Groag, and Karen M. Offen. 1983. *Women, the Family, and Freedom*. Vol. 2. Stanford: Stanford University Press.

Benjamin, Walter. 1978. *Reflections*. New York: Harcourt Brace Jovanovich.

Bennett, Tony. 1988. "The Exhibitionary Complex." *New Formations* 4 (Spring): 73–102.

Benoist, Alain de. 1993–94. "The Idea of Empire." *Telos* 98–99 (Winter–Spring): 81–98.

Béranger, Henry. 1937. "Avant-propos." In *L'Empire colonial français à l'Ile des Cygnes*. Marseille: Saroul.

Berstein, Serge. 1988. *La France des années 30*. Paris: Armand Colin.

Betts, Raymond F. 1961. *Assimilation and Association in French Colonial Theory, 1890–1914*. New York: Columbia University Press.

——. 1991. *France and Decolonisation, 1900–1960*. London: Macmillan.

Bhabha, Homi. 1994. *The Location of Culture*. London: Routledge.

Bonnet, J.-C. 1976. *Les Pouvoirs publics français et l'immigration dans l'entre-deux-guerres*. Lyon. [Citation posted on the Internet by Clifford Rosenberg.]

Borelly, René. 1931. *Promenade à l'Exposition coloniale*. Paris: L'Association de maîtres imprimeurs.

Borne, Dominique, and Henri Dubief. 1989. *La Crise des années 30*. Paris: Seuil.

Breton, André. 1967. *La Clé des champs*. Utrecht: Pauvert.

——. 1972. *Manifestoes of Surrealism*. Trans. Richard Seaver and Helen R. Lane. Ann Arbor: University of Michigan Press.

——. 1985. *Manifestes du surréalisme*. Paris: Gallimard.

Brotchie, Alastair, Malcolm Green et al., eds. 1987. *Raymond Roussel: Life, Death, and Works*. London: Atlas.

Brubaker, Rogers. 1992. *Citizenship and Nationhood in France and Germany*. Cambridge: Harvard University Press.

Caburet, Bernard. 1968. *Raymond Roussel*. Paris: Seghers.

Caillois, Roger. 1950. *L'Homme et le sacré*. Paris: Gallimard.

Capatti, Alberto. 1989. *Le Goût du nouveau*. Paris: Albin Michel.

Caradec, François. 1972. *Vie de Raymond Roussel, 1877–1933*. [Paris]: Pauvert.

Carassou, Michel. 1985. "L'Afrique de René Crevel." *Europe* 670–80 (Nov.–Dec.): 11–15.

——. 1989. *René Crevel*. Paris: Fayard.

Carrel, Alexis. 1968. *L'Homme, cet inconnu*. Paris: Plon.

Ce qu'il faut voir à l'Exposition coloniale. 1931. Lille: Les Presses de la Société N.E.A.

Cendrars, Blaise. 1993. *Du monde entier*. Paris: Gallimard.

Césaire, Aimé. 1955. *Discours sur le colonialisme*. Paris: Présence Africaine.

Chénieux-Gendron, Jacqueline. 1983. *Le Surréalisme et le roman, 1922–1950*. Lausanne: L'Age d'homme.

Clifford, James. 1986. "On Ethnographic Allegory." In *Writing Culture*, ed. James Clifford and George E. Marcus, 98–121. Berkeley: University of California Press.

——. 1988. *The Predicament of Culture*. Cambridge: Harvard University Press.

——. 1994. "Negrophilia." In *A New History of French Literature*, ed. Denis Hollier, 901–8. Cambridge: Harvard University Press.

Collomb, Michel, ed. 1993. *Paul Morand, écrivain*. Montpellier: Université Paul Valéry.

Coquery-Vidrovitch, Catherine, and Charles-Robert Ageron. 1991. *Histoire de la France coloniale*. Vol. 3. Paris: Armand Colin.

Courtot, Claude. 1969. *René Crevel*. Paris: Seghers.

Crevel, René. 1925. "Le Music-Hall et les cirques." *La Revue européenne* 34 (Dec. 1): 64–66.

——. 1929. *Êtes-vous fous?* Paris: Gallimard.

——. 1966. *Le Clavecin de Diderot*. Paris: Pauvert. Originally published 1932.

——. 1974. *Mon Corps et moi*. Paris: Pauvert. Originally published 1926.

——. 1975. *Babylone*. Paris: Pauvert. Originally published 1927.

——. 1986. *L'Esprit contre la raison et autres écrits surréalistes*. Paris: Société Nouvelle des Éditions Pauvert. Originally published 1927.

——. 1996. *Babylon*. Trans. Kay Boyle. Los Angeles: Sun and Moon Press.

Criel, Gaston. 1954. Untitled piece in *Temps mêlés*, nos. 10–11 (special issue on René Crevel).

Crowder, Michael. 1969. "The Administration of West Africa." *Tarikh* 2 (4): 59–71.

De Jough, James. 1990. *Vicious Modernism: Black Harlem and the Literary Imagination*. Cambridge: Cambridge University Press.

De Man, Paul. 1979a. *Allegories of Reading: Figural Language in Rousseau, Nietzsche, Rilke, and Proust*. New Haven: Yale University Press.

——. 1979b. "Semiology and Rhetoric." In *Textual Strategies*, ed. Josué V. Harari., 121–40. Ithaca: Cornell University Press.

Deleuze, Gilles, and Félix Guattari. 1989. *Anti-Oedipus*. Trans. Robert Hurley, Mark Seem, and Helen R. Lane. Minneapolis: University of Minnesota Press.

Deloncle, Pierre. 1931. "La Continuité de l'action coloniale française." *L'Illustration* 4603, May 23.

Derakhshesh, Derayeh. 1990. " 'Les Noirs' dans les oeuvres de Paul Morand." *Cla* 33 (June): 394–401.

Derrida, Jacques. 1976. *Of Grammatology*. Trans. Gayatri Chakravorty Spivak. Baltimore: Johns Hopkins University Press.

——. 1985. "Des Tours de Babel." In *L'Art des confins: Mélanges offerts à Maurice de Gandillac*, ed. Annie Cazenave and Jean-François Lyotard, 209–37. Paris: Presses Universitaires de France.

Derys, Gaston. 1929. *L'Art d'être gourmand*. Paris: Albin Michel.

Diderot, Denis, and Jean Le Rond d'Alembert, eds. 1966. *Encyclopédie ou Dictionnaire raisonné des sciences, des arts et des métiers*. Vols. 4 and 7. Stuttgart-Bad Cannstatt: Friedrich Frommann. Originally published in 1757.

Dupays, Paul. 1938. *Voyages autour du monde: Pavillons étrangers et pavillons coloniaux à l'Exposition de 1937*. Paris: Henri Didier.

Durosay, Daniel. 1993. "Marc Allégret ou les débuts absolus." In *CinéMémoire*, ed. Emmanuelle Toulet and Christian Belaygue, 194–97. Paris: Cinémathèque française.

Dyer, Richard, and Ginette Vincendeau, eds. 1992. *Popular European Cinema*. London: Routledge.

Eliade, Mircea. 1957. *Mythes, rêves et mystères*. Paris: Gallimard.

Elias, Norbert. 1978. *The Civilizing Process: The History of Manners*. Trans. Edmund Jephcott. New York: Urizen.

L'Empire Colonial Français à l'Ile des Cygnes. 1937. Marseille: Saroul.

Exposition internationale des arts et techniques: Rapport général. Tome 8, vol. 2. 1938. Paris: Imprimerie Nationale.

Exposition internationale des arts et techniques, Paris 1937: Guide officiel. 1937. Paris: Société pour le développement du Tourisme.

Ezra, Elizabeth, ed. 1993. *Histoires coloniales*. Special issue of *Diacritics* 23 (Fall).

Fabian, Johannes. 1993. *Time and the Other*. New York: Columbia University Press.

Fanon, Frantz. 1967. *Black Skin, White Masks*. New York: Grove Press.

Fayol, Henri. 1979. *Administration industrielle et générale*. Paris: Bordas. Originally published in 1916.

Ferro, Marc. 1997. *Colonization*. London: Routledge.

Ferry, Jean. 1953. *Une étude sur Raymond Roussel*. Saverne: Arcanes.

Fineman, Joel. 1981. "The Structure of Allegorical Desire." In *Allegory and Representation*, ed. Stephen J. Greenblatt, 26–60. Baltimore: Johns Hopkins University Press.

Foucault, Michel. 1975. *Surveiller et punir: Naissance de la prison*. Paris: Gallimard.

——. 1979. *Discipline and Punish: The Birth of the Prison*. Trans. Alan Sheridan. New York: Vintage.

Freud, Sigmund. [1950]. *Totem and Taboo*. Trans. James Strachey. New York: Norton.

——. 1966. *Introductory Lectures on Psychoanalysis*. Trans. James Strachey. New York: Norton.

——. 1967. *Beyond the Pleasure Principle*. Trans. James Strachey. New York: Bantam.

——. 1978. *Totem und Tabu*. In *Gesammelte Werke*, vol. 9. Frankfurt am Main: Fischer.

——. 1981. *The Standard Edition*. Trans. James Strachey. London: Hogarth Press.

——. 1989. *Five Lectures on Psycho-Analysis*. Trans. James Strachey. New York: Norton.

Gates, Henry Louis, Jr. 1986. *"Race," Writing, and Difference*. Chicago: University of Chicago Press.

Gaudemar, Jean-Paul de. 1979. *La Mobilisation générale*. Paris: Champ Urbain.

——. 1982. *L'Ordre et la production: Naissance et formes de la discipline d'usine*. Paris: Dunod.

Genette, Gérard. 1969. *Figures III*. Paris: Seuil.

George, G. L. 1934. "Josephine Baker revient à l'écran." *Pour Vous* (Sept. 27): 7.

Girard, René. 1972. *La Violence et le sacré*. Paris: Grasset.

——. 1977. *The Violence and the Sacred*. Trans. Patrick Gregory. Baltimore: Johns Hopkins University Press.

Girardet, Raoul. 1972. *L'Idée coloniale en France de 1871 à 1962*. Paris: Hachette.

Gobineau, Joseph-Arthur de. 1940. *Essai sur l'inégalité des races humaines*. Paris: Firmin-Didot. Originally published in 1853.

——. 1970. *Gobineau: Selected Political Writings*. Ed. Michael D. Biddiss. Trans. Brian Nelson. London: Jonathan Cape.

Goldberg, David Theo. 1993. *Racist Culture*. Cambridge: Blackwell.

Green, André. 1972. "Cannibalisme: Réalité ou phantasme agi?" *Nouvelle Revue de Psychanalyse* 6 (Fall): 27–52.

Greenhalgh, Paul. 1988. *Ephemeral Vistas*. Manchester: Manchester University Press.

Guitard-Auviste, Ginette. 1981. *Paul Morand*. Paris: Hachette.

Halbwachs, Maurice. 1950. *La Mémoire collective*. Paris: Presses Universitaires de France.

Hamacher, Werner, Neil Hertz, and Thomas Keenan, eds. 1989. *Responses: On Paul de Man's Wartime Journalism*. Lincoln: University of Nebraska Press.

Hamon, Philippe. 1992. *Expositions: Literature and Architecture in Nineteenth-Century France*. Trans. Katia Sainson-Frank and Lisa Maguire. Berkeley: University of California Press.

Haney, Lynn. 1981. *Naked at the Feast: A Biography of Josephine Baker*. New York: Dodd, Mead.

Hayward, Susan. 1993. *French National Cinema*. London: Routledge.

Hodeir, Catherine. 1983. "L'Épopée de la décolonisation à travers les expositions universelles du XXe siècle." *Le Livre des expositions universelles, 1851–1989*. Paris: Union Centrale des Arts décoratifs.

——. 1984. "Une journée à l'Exposition coloniale." *L'Histoire*, no. 69: 41–48.

——. 1987. "La France d'Outre-mer." In *Cinquantenaire de l'Exposition internationale des arts et des techniques dans la vie moderne*. Paris: Institut Français d'Architecture.

Hodeir, Catherine, and Michel Pierre. 1991. *L'Exposition coloniale*. Brussels: Editions Complexe.

Hollier, Denis, ed. 1994. *A New History of French Literature*. Cambridge: Harvard University Press.

Houppermans, Sjef. 1985. *Raymond Roussel: Écriture et désir*. [Paris]: José Corti.

Hutton, Patrick H. 1988. "Collective Memory and Collective Mentalities: The Halbwachs-Ariès Connection." *Historical Reflections / Réflexions Historiques* 15 (Summer): 311–22.

Jameson, Fredric. 1981. *The Political Unconscious*. Ithaca: Cornell University Press.

JanMohamed, Abdul R. 1986. "The Economy of Manichean Allegory: The Function of Racial Difference in Colonialist Literature." In *Race, "Writing," and Difference*, ed. Henry Louis Gates, Jr., 78–106. Chicago: University of Chicago Press.

Jean, Marcel, and Arpad Mezei. 1950. *Genèse de la pensée moderne*. Paris: Corrêa.

Joseph, Richard A. 1975. "The German Question in French Cameroun, 1919–1939." *Comparative Studies in Society and History* 17 (Jan.): 65–90.

Jourdain, Francis. 1936. *Faut-il donner des colonies à Hitler?* Paris: Publications du Comité mondial contre la guerre et le fascisme.

Kaplan, Alice Yaeger. 1986. *Reproductions of Banality: Fascism, Literature, and French Intellectual Life*. Minneapolis: University of Minnesota Press.

Kear, Jon. 1996. "Vénus noire: Joséphine Baker and the Parisian Music-Hall." In *Parisian Fields*, ed. Michael Sheringham, 46–70. London: Reaktion Books.

Klein, Melanie. 1948. "A Contribution to the Theory of Anxiety and Guilt." *International Journal of Psycho-Analysis*, no. 29: 114–23.

Kristeva, Julia. 1978. *Sémeiotiké: Recherches pour une sémanalyse*. Paris: Seuil.

——. 1991. *Strangers to Ourselves*. Trans. Leon S. Roudiez. New York: Columbia University Press.

——. 1993. *Nations without Nationalism*. Trans. Leon S. Roudiez. New York: Columbia University Press.

Lagny, Michèle, Marie-Claire Ropars, and Pierre Sorlin. 1986. *Générique des années trente*. Paris: PUF.

Lange, Robert. 1937. *Merveilles de l'Exposition de 1937*. Paris: Denoël.

Larousse du XXe siècle. 1928. Paris: Librairie Larousse.

Lebovics, Herman. 1989–90. "Donner à voir l'Empire colonial: L'Exposition coloniale internationale de Paris en 1931." *Gradhiva*, no. 7 (Winter): 18–28.

——. 1994. *True France*. Ithaca: Cornell University Press.

Le Goff, Jacques. 1988. *Histoire et mémoire*. Paris: Gallimard.

Leiris, Michel. 1964. "Le Voyageur et son ombre." Bizarre 34–35.

——. 1992. *Zébrage*. Paris: Gallimard.

Lelieur, Anne-Claude, and Raymond Bachollet, eds. 1985. *François Kollar: La France Travaille, Regard sur les années trente*. Paris: Mairie de Paris.

Leprun, Sylviane. 1989. "Paysages de la France extérieure: La mise en scène des colonies à l'Exposition du centenaire." *Le Mouvement social* 149 (Oct.–Dec.): 99–128.

Lévi-Strauss, Claude. 1962. *Le Totémisme aujourd'hui*. Paris: Presses Universitaires de France.

——. 1964. *Le Cru et le cuit*. Paris: Plon.

——. 1971. *L'Homme nu*. Paris: Plon.

——. 1973. *Anthropologie structurale*. Paris: Plon.

——. 1977. *Tristes Tropiques*. Trans. John and Doreen Weightman. New York: Pocket Books.

——. 1979a. *The Origin of Table Manners*. Trans. John and Doreen Weightman. New York: Harper Colophon.

——. 1979b. *Myth and Meaning*. New York: Schocken.

——. 1987. *Race et histoire*. Paris: Denoël. Originally published in 1952.

Lévy-Bruhl, Lucien. 1960. *La Mentalité primitive*. Paris: Presses Universitaires de France.

Lewis, Martin Deming. 1962. "One Hundred Million Frenchmen: The 'Assimilation' Theory in French Colonial Policy." *Comparative Studies in Society and History* 4 (Jan.): 129–53.

Le Livre des expositions universelles, 1851–1989. 1983. Paris: Union Centrale des Arts décoratifs.

Le Livre d'or officiel de l'Exposition internationale des arts et techniques dans la vie moderne. 1938. Paris: SPEC.

Lovejoy, A. O. 1948. *Essays in the History of Ideas*. Baltimore: Johns Hopkins University Press.

Louvrier, Pascal, and Eric Canal-Forgues. 1994. *Paul Morand: Le sourire du hara-kiri*. Paris: Librairie Académique Perrin.

MacCannell, Dean. 1976. *The Tourist: A New Theory of the Leisure Class*. New York: Schocken.

Marrus, Michael R., and Robert O. Paxton. 1981. *Vichy France and the Jews*. New York: Basic Books.

Matthews, J. H. 1966. *Surrealism and the Novel*. Ann Arbor: University of Michigan Press.

Memmi, Albert. 1970. *The Colonizer and the Colonized*. Trans. Howard Greenfeld. Boston: Beacon Press.

——. 1985. *Portrait du colonisé*. Paris: Gallimard.

Metz, Christian. 1984. *Le Signifiant imaginaire: Psychanalyse et cinéma*. [Cher]: Christian Bourgois.

Miller, Christopher L. 1985. *Blank Darkness: Africanist Discourse in French*. Chicago: University of Chicago Press.

Moneta, Jacob. 1971. *La Politique du Parti Communiste français dans la question coloniale, 1920–1963*. Paris: Maspero.

Montagnon, Pierre. 1988. *La France coloniale*. Paris: Pygmalion / Gérard Watelet.

Montaigne, Michel de. 1950. *Essais*. Ed. A. Thibaudet. Paris: Gallimard.

Morand, Paul. 1929. *Hiver Caraïbe*. Paris: Flammarion.

——. 1931. *Papiers d'identité*. Paris: Grasset.

——. 1934. *France-la-doulce*. Paris: Gallimard.

——. 1981. *Oeuvres*. Paris: Flammarion.

——. 1988. *New York*. Paris: Fiammarion. Originally published 1930.

——. 1989. *Magie Noire*. Paris: Grasset. Originally published 1928.

——. 1992. *Nouvelles complètes*. Ed. Michel Collomb. Paris: Gallimard.

Mulvey, Laura. 1986. "Visual Pleasure and Narrative Cinema." In *Narrative, Apparatus, Ideology*, ed. Philip Rosen, 198–209. New York: Columbia University Press.

——. 1989. "Afterthoughts on 'Visual Pleasure and Narrative Cinema' inspired by *Duel in the Sun*." In *Visual and Other Pleasures*, 29–39. London: Macmillan.

Nadeau, Maurice. 1964. *Histoire du surréalisme*. Paris: Seuil.

Nicoll, Edna L., with Suzanne Flour. 1931. *A Travers l'Exposition coloniale*. Paris: Editions Edna Nicoll.

Nignon, Edouard. [1926]. *Les Plaisirs de la table*. Paris: Meynial.

——. 1933. *Eloges de la cuisine française*. Paris: Piazza.

Nora, Pierre, ed. 1984. *Les Lieux de mémoire*. Vol. 1. *La République*. Paris: Gallimard.

——. 1996. *Realms of Memory: The Construction of the French Past*. Vol. 1. *Conflicts and Divisions*. Trans. Arthur Goldhammer. New York: Columbia University Press.

Norindr, Panivong. 1996. *Phantasmatic Indochina*. Durham: Duke University Press.

Olivier, Marcel. 1931. "L'Exposition coloniale oeuvre de Paix." *L'Illustration* 4603 (May 23).

——. 1933. *Exposition coloniale 1931: Rapport général.* Vol. 5. Paris: Imprimerie nationale.

Orwell, George. 1969. "Marrakech." In *The Collected Essays, Journals, and Letters of George Orwell*, vol. 1. Ed. Sonia Orwell and Ian Angus. London: Secker and Warburg, 387–93.

Ory, Pascal. 1982. *Les Expositions universelles de Paris.* [Paris]: Ramsay.

Palà, Sylvie. 1981. *Documents Exposition coloniale internationale.* Paris: Bibliothèques de la Ville de Paris.

Raillard, Georges. 1984. "Le Tissu du billard." *Revue des Sciences Humaines* 1 (193): 77–95.

Rapport du Premier Congrès Latin d'Eugénique. 1937. Paris: Masson et Cie.

Raymond, François. 1988. "Raymond Roussel et le récit d'énigme." *Europe* 714 (Oct.): 121–30.

Rebérioux, Madeleine. 1989. "Au tournant des expos: 1889." *Le Mouvement social* 149 (Oct.–Dec.): 3–13.

Renan, Ernest. 1947–61. *Oeuvres complètes.* Vol. 1. Paris: Calmann-Lévy.

Ricoeur, Paul, C. Larre, R. Panikkar, and A. Kagame. 1975. *Les Cultures et le temps.* Paris: Payot.

Rochester, Myrna Bell. 1978. *René Crevel: Le Pays des miroirs absolus.* Saratoga: Anma Libri.

Rodowick, David. 1982. "The Difficulty of Difference." *Wide Angle* 5 (1): 4–15.

Ross, Kristin. 1996. *Fast Cars, Clean Bodies: Decolonization and the Reordering of French Culture.* Cambridge: MIT Press.

Roussel, Raymond. 1927. *La Poussière de soleils.* Paris: Lemerre.

——. 1963a. *L'Étoile au front.* [Paris]: Pauvert. Originally published 1925.

——. 1963b. *Impressions d'Afrique.* Paris: Pauvert. Originally published 1910.

——. 1965. *Locus Solus.* Paris: Pauvert. Originally published in 1914.

——. 1994. *La Seine.* Ed. Patrick Besnier. Paris: Pauvert.

——. 1995. *Comment j'ai écrit certains de mes livres.* Paris: Pauvert. Originally published in 1932.

Rousso, Henry. 1991. *The Vichy Syndrome: History and Memory in France since 1944.* Trans. Arthur Goldhammer. Cambridge: Harvard University Press.

Said, Edward. 1979. *Orientalism.* New York: Random House.

Sarkany, Stéphane. 1968. *Paul Morand et le cosmopolitisme littéraire.* Paris: Klincksieck.

Schneider, William H. 1990a. "The Eugenics Movement in France, 1890–1940." In *The Wellborn Science*, ed. Mark B. Adams. New York: Oxford University Press.

——. 1990b. *Quality and Quantity: The Quest for Biological Regeneration in Twentieth-Century France.* Cambridge: Cambridge University Press.

Shattuck, Roger. 1986. *The Innocent Eye.* New York: Washington Square Press.

Silverman, Maxim. 1992. *Deconstructing the Nation: Immigration, Racism, and Citizenship in Modern France.* London: Routledge.

Soupault, Philippe. 1981 and 1986. *Mémoires de l'oubli.* Vols. 1 and 2. Paris: Lachenal & Ritter.

Stacey, Jackie. 1992. "Desperately Seeking Difference." In *The Sexual Subject*, 244–57. London: Routledge.

Stovall, Tyler. 1996. *Paris Noir: African Americans in the City of Light*. New York: Houghton Mifflin.

Suret-Canale, Jean. 1971. *French Colonialism in Tropical Africa, 1900–1945*. Trans. Till Gottheiner. New York: Pica.

Taguieff, Pierre-André. 1993–94. "From Race to Culture: The New Right's View of European Identity." *Telos* 98–99 (Winter–Spring): 99–125.

Thalmann, Rita, ed. 1986. *Femmes et fascismes*. Paris: Tierce.

Tharaud, Jérome, and Jean Tharaud. 1931. "Les Pavillons des Missions." *L'Illustration 4603* (May 23).

Thirion, André. 1975. *Revolutionaries without Revolution*. Trans. Joachim Neugroschel. New York: Macmillan.

Thomarel, André. 1937. "La France d'Outre-mer à l'Exposition de 1937." Unpaginated supplement. *Le Courrier Colonial* (Nov. 26).

Tracts surréalistes et déclarations collectives (1922 / 1969). 1980. Vol. 1. Paris: Le Terrain vague.

Vallin, Paul. 1987. *Les "Frances" d'Outre-mer*. Paris: La Pensée universelle.

Van Vechten, Carl. 1927. *Le Paradis des nègres*. Trans. J. Sabouraud. Paris: Kra.

Vincendeau, Ginette. 1985. "French Cinema in the 1930s: Social Text and Context of a Popular Entertainment Medium." Ph.D. dissertation, University of East Anglia.

Vivier de Streel, M. du (Membre du Conseil supérieur des colonies). 1932. *Les Enseignements généraux de l'Exposition coloniale*.

Index

Abel, Richard, 105
Affaire du foulard, 20, 151
Africanist discourse, 9–10, 115, 124–25. *See also* Miller, Christopher
Algeria, xii, 2, 21
  centennial celebration of conquest, 3
  and l'Étoile nord-africaine, 2
  war of independence, 10
  See also Maghreb
Allégret, Marc
  and *Le Voyage au Congo*, 2
  and *Zouzou*, 2, 100
Ambivalence, colonial, 5, 7, 8, 9, 10, 11, 17, 19, 76. *See also* Bhabha, Homi
American culture. *See* United States of America
Anderson, Benedict, 109, 110
Andrew, Dudley, 102–3, 104, 106
Angkor Wat, 14–15, 28
Antisemitism, xiii, xiv, 43, 107, 108, 139, 144, 159n.3
Aragon, Louis, 76
  and *Exposition anticoloniale*, 27
Artaud, Antonin
  and the *Exposition coloniale internationale*, 3
Assimilation, xii, 4–7, 8, 10–11, 16, 17, 19, 20, 37, 43, 46, 50, 54, 56, 61, 77, 100, 101, 107, 110, 112, 113, 115, 123, 124, 125, 127, 130, 133, 134, 140, 141, 149, 152, 153
  compared to association, 4–6, 19, 43, 46, 50
Association, 4, 5, 6, 13, 19, 43, 46, 50
Atlantide, L' (film), 3
Augé, Marc, 91, 95
Automatic writing, 76

Baker, Josephine, 2, 8, 9, 19, 97–138, 129
  in *Princesse Tam-Tam*, 99, 100, 113–28, 152
  in *Zouzou*, 99, 100–113, 152
Balandier, Georges, 6
Balibar, Etienne, 10, 20
Barthes, Roland, 82
Bataille, Georges, 131
Beauty contests. *See Miss France d'Outre-Mer*
Benjamin, Walter, 23
Bennett, Tony, 32–33
Benoist, Alain de, 151
Benoît, Pierre, 3
Bhaba, Homi, 7–8, 17, 110
Birthrate. *See Dénatalité*
Blum, Léon, 29. *See also* Popular Front
Brubaker, Rogers, 149
Breton, André, 27, 48, 64, 76, 131
British empire. *See* Great Britain

DATE DUE

APR 2 4 2001			
MAR 2 4 2001			
NOV 0 5 2003			

Demco, Inc. 38-293